WRITING
FOR THE
MARKETS

WRITING
FOR THE
MARKETS

David Raffelock

FUNK & WAGNALLS · NEW YORK

To Esse,
who gave meaning to my life

Preface

This book was written with the thought of bringing a greater degree of harmony between editors and writers. Many writers feel that editors are antagonistic toward them or are indifferent to the work they submit. I think this delusion may be dispelled after one reads the interested and constructive information and advice so freely offered by editors.

Acknowledgment is made to the many editors and publishers in all fields in which original manuscripts are used for their generous cooperation in answering our questionnaires; in many instances they sent a separate letter to explain more fully their needs and their gripes, and to give their encouragement.

Without the cooperation of the National Writers Club (745 Sherman Street, Denver, Colorado) and my wife, this book could not have been written.

DAVID RAFFELOCK

Contents

1

Know Your Markets

You write "The End" to your manuscript and sigh with relief. "Well, that's a piece done and I think it is good—as good as lots of stuff the magazines are printing today."

It's always a satisfying feeling when you've finished a manuscript, be it a filler, a full-length story, or a book. But now that the job is done where shall it be sent? Considering the amount of thought and work you put into it, just any old magazine isn't good enough. Start at the top and work down, if necessary. *Saturday Evening Post* or *Redbook*, you've heard, pay the highest rates, so why not give them a try first? If they don't take it, you can see it in print even if it means sending the manuscript to the confessions or the juvenile magazines. One cent a word is better than nothing.

This hypothetical writer means well by his "creation," and you cannot blame him for wanting to get as much for his work as he can. Even if he's a gifted writer, however, he is almost doomed to disappointment by such hit-or-miss marketing. Today magazines and most other users of manuscripts specialize, and therefore unenlightened marketing is largely futile. Anyone who thinks that any two magazines are as alike as two peas in a pod is as wrong as this comparison is trite.

Any emphasis at this point on writing for magazines, rather than for other media, is purely intentional, because most aspiring writers turn first to magazines when trying to make a sale. Nevertheless, *all* markets for manuscripts will be considered and evaluated for their receptiveness to unsolicited free-lance submissions.

Many a person is tempted to write because advertised writers' services often make much of the fact that there are more than twenty-five hundred literary markets in the United States. Surely, when there are that many buyers of manuscripts, an article can be sold to one of them.

There was a time, forty or fifty years ago, when a writer could seclude himself in his ivory tower and write "for his own amazement," and then try as many as six to ten logical markets, any one of which might take his manuscript. Not so today. Consider any two women's magazines, for instance: Each has a distinctive policy and requires a slant peculiar to that magazine. When you consider other types of magazines, differentiations become even more marked and varied. No wonder editors universally plead with writers, as does Richard Kaplan, associate editor of *Redbook*, when he urges, "Read the magazine! We get so many suggestions for stories we have just done, or stories we wouldn't do in a million years."

The author who fails to heed this advice will spend a

lot of money on envelopes and postage until maybe, by pure chance, he happens to match his manuscript with just the right magazine. When I started free-lance writing, the "pulps," those writers' friends, all-fiction magazines printed on pulp paper, were in the ascendancy. My first stories brought comments such as this from editors: "You wrote a good story, but it's too psychological for our readers." When I began to read *Ace High*, *Western Stories*, *Top Notch*, and the others, instead of merely noting the titles, I made sales. Sometimes it's a hard lesson to learn.

Some media depend almost entirely on unsolicited, free-lance submissions, whereas others do not even open an envelope containing a manuscript. Knowledge is power; this applies to your writing too. It gives you the power to get acceptances instead of rejection slips.

First of all, it should be borne in mind that there are no "easy" markets. Many persons, some of them knowledgeable and skillful, are writing today. Editors don't have to compromise on just anything to fill their books; they don't have to rewrite, though a few still do. Even the markets most avid for new writers have a wide selection from which to choose. Some magazines receive more than 25,000 manuscripts a year; that's at least 2,000 a month, 500 a week. That's competition!

Competition never scared off anyone who really wants to write. And neither do rejection slips. Charles Booth wrote and tried to sell 105 stories before one was bought. John Creasey, the novelist, started writing when he was nineteen, a tender age at which to begin to reap rejections (750 of them) before he finally sold a mystery story four years later. Philip Stong, author of *State Fair* and other novels, wrote and sent out 13 books before he sold one. A prize for persistence goes to Ben Lucien Burman, who doggedly mailed the same story 44 times before it finally sold. Fortitude—the ability to accept rejection slips—is one of the first requirements of the professional writer. However, there are short cuts, and I will tell you how to make your manuscript stand out like a miniskirt at a square dance, thereby increasing its chances of selling.

Rule Number One is: Put a happy face on your manuscript. Some of them scowl, turning the editor against them from the moment they are glanced at. These are the manuscripts that are typed with a faint ribbon, pockmarked by messy erasures, wrinkled by pen-scratched interpolations. The first sentence of such a submission must be so impressive that it overshadows the sloppy appearance of the manuscript—and a sentence of this caliber is as rare as rates at $20 a word, even among skilled professionals.

Anyone can prepare a presentable manuscript. All that's required are pride in your work and a freedom from the parsimony that keeps some writers from buying a fairly good grade of paper and a new ribbon. That's a large order for some, but they are asking for rejection slips. You don't *need* to be in their class.

Speaking of rejection slips. The most prevalent is the printed form that says, "Thank you for letting us see this manuscript. We are sorry that it does not meet our present needs." This form doesn't tell you anything about why your manuscript was returned or how you might alter it for resubmission. Some writers think that a magazine or book publisher ought to have various types of rejection slips: one that says, in effect, that the submitted script is lousy, a candidate for the wastebasket (if the editor had the courage to drop it distastefully there); another that gives the writer an honest appraisal while pointing out that the manuscript is not top grade but that if the author keeps plugging away he might be published; a third that provides encouragement, telling the writer that truly he came close to gaining an acceptance and should keep trying.

As a matter of fact, there *are* three types of rejections. There is the all too familiar nondescript one quoted in the foregoing paragraph; it purposely says nothing, dismissing the writer politely and with as little friction as possible. The second kind is the same rejection slip, but with a word or more written on, such as "Sorry" or "Try us again." When you get those precious comments, you know that you have sincerely interested an editor in your work. As Naomi Lewis, fiction editor of *Good Housekeeping,* wrote me: "If the would-be writer has sent *GH* ten short stories over a period of time on a variety of subjects, and has never had as much as a 'sorry' on the rejection card, he had better accept the fact that he is not coming anywhere near hitting our market."

The third kind is the personally typed letter to you. This may be noncommittal, too, in that it offers no criticisms, but it does say that your work has created editorial interest and the editor would like to see more of your material. Editors don't have time to write letters; when they do write, the encouragement is intended and real. A writer on the ball will see to it that this editor gets to see more of his *good* work.

Time was when editors such as Ray Long wrote rejection letters and passed out good advice to struggling writers. The population explosion, which spawned an

ever-increasing number of would-be writers, has put an
end to that. A few magazines in the "good old days"
used what were called "informative rejection slips,"
printed forms with boxes that could be checked to
point out shortcomings in the submitted piece. These,
too, have gone the way of many other pre-space-age
mores. Editors now say they are not running a school
for writers; they have no time for or interest in trying
to teach writers. You have to develop fortitude and be
as professional as you can in your marketing. This is
vital to avoiding rejection slips.

Although some writers immediately strike out for the
august literary magazines or the leading "slicks,"
others, more realistic or perhaps merely more modest,
are content to cut their eyeteeth on magazines that
offer little if any competition from the successful pros.
Such men as Nobel Prize-winner Sinclair Lewis, whose
first sale consisted of a joke, or Joseph Hergesheimer,
whose first sale was a recipe for stuffed cabbage, did not
disdain any market while trying to make the grade with
bigger stuff.

MARKETS IN WHICH COMPETITION IS NOT SEVERE

Juvenile Magazine. The religious juveniles rely heavily
on free-lancers. Payment ranges from one-half cent a
word to five cents, the latter only infrequently. Obviously, the writer who can earn upwards of $1,000 for a
script isn't going into competition with you in this market. The lay juveniles range from Johnnies-come-lately
that pay two or three cents a word to those that are

well established and pay as much as $800 for a manuscript.

Religious Magazine. Rates in this group usually are low, so editors look to the "over the transom" manuscripts for their material. With proper specialization, you can sell to them, especially those that represent your particular religion or sect.

Trade Journal. As with most market groups, generalities here are difficult to make. Some of these publications are so highly specialized and demanding that only experienced trade writers can expect to sell to them. On the other hand, there exists no larger group of editors who are so willing to work with a writer, shaping his work, directing him so that he may become a steady contributor.

Literary Magazine. This amazingly varied and complex group provides a market for almost anything from the fundamentalist to the psychedelic. Because most of them do not pay for material, many inexperienced writers think that these magazines are an "open sesame" to publication. A few are, but most require a high degree of originality and skill. Their receptiveness to new writers is unstinted. Except for a few of the more august "little" magazines and quarterlies, there is virtually no preference for established writers.

Greeting Card. The seeming simplicity of writing verse or prose for this market attracts many aspiring writers. It may not be difficult to make sales if the writer will study what now is on the racks so that he may avoid repeating what already has been done. Some greeting card companies buy frequently from the unsolicited mail. Encouragement is given to writers who show promise.

WHERE COMPETITION IS STRONGER

Confession Story Magazine. This group professes to use stories based upon actual happenings. Here as nowhere else, "the story's the thing." Highly stylized writing is frowned upon as seeming to come from professional writers rather than from the true "confessors." This wide-open market is avid for material from adept writers.

Men's Magazine. Some of these, paying modest rates, are "easier" markets for those who can inject the right appeal into their material, whether or not their writing style is distinguishable as such. Others that pay better can command the attention of well-known writers.

Consumer Magazine. This classification is extremely broad, ranging from the high-circulation family magazines to those that cater to a segment of the population. There is not much chance for the beginner to sell to the highest-paying of these, but because of the diversity of publications included in this area, some of the consumer magazines, those of limited circulation and a low word-rate, offer a more receptive market for the freelance writer.

Specialized and Technical Magazine. Editors of these publications are standing at the door, ready to entice a likely customer. These magazines, representing involved technical subjects, hobbies, sports, science, *et al.,* need material, but they are lukewarm to any contributor who is not an authority (or seems to be).

Opinion and Educational Magazine. Almost everyone knows how to run the country, wipe out crime, or bring up children. If you are a recognized authority you can gain a hearing, but if you're not, it's best to confine your efforts to "Letters to the Editor" of your local newspaper.

Book. Despite "going public" and seemingly putting money before art, book publishers are aware that the new writer is vital to them. Anyone who can write interestingly about a subject not already exploited to death will get a sympathetic hearing. It may be more difficult for the novelist, but no publisher will refuse a writer a hearing. It is necessary to gain skill as a writer before knocking on the doors of publishers.

MARKETS IN WHICH COMPETITION IS SEVERE

Stage Play. Although Broadway producers will consider a free-lance manuscript submitted directly or through an agent, reports usually are slow and uncertain. Broadway (and off-Broadway) has no "welcome" sign out for new writers. The way to production (and it, too, is rough) is via the little theater or amateur thespian groups.

Newspaper Syndicate. The decreasing number of newspapers has severely constricted the possibilities of getting a new column or continuing feature started. What actual demand there is looks toward a nationally-known figure. The only door that won't close on your foot is the small-town weekly newspaper, if you're willing to write for peanuts—or maybe only the shells.

MARKETS CLOSED TO DIRECT SUBMISSIONS

Motion Picture. Most movie studios return unopened any envelope that seems to contain a manuscript. A middleman is the *sine qua non* here; not only must you have an agent, he must be recognized.

Television. This hungry, and often lean, market seeks material, but only if you've got an agent. If you can get one who is a member of the Society of Authors' Representatives, you'll have the studios standing up to greet you. Just any agent, especially of the sort that advertises, won't get you inside the reception room.

Song. There is no use in sending a song to the big popular song publishers; the envelope will be stamped "Refused," and back it will come. A few smaller song publishers, especially those issuing novelty or religious songs, may give you a hearing.

Now let's look into these and other markets more thoroughly and see what makes them tick—and how to make sure your mail contains checks instead of rejection slips.

2

The Juvenile Magazine Market

The easiest thing in the world is to write for kids. For the little tykes all you have to do is use simple language and one-syllable words. If you are writing for the older ones, you don't have to worry about having a fresh plot, for they haven't had a chance yet to read much, so just about anything is new to them.

If you think that, you're sure to earn a fast rejection slip. You have to get past the editor before you can reach children, and editors have definite ideas about what is interesting and appropriate.

Bob Fischer, editor of *Teen, Keen Teen, Teen Pix, Teenville,* and *Cool,* puts it this way, "Remember that teenagers are brighter than you think. Create imaginative writing that is not stereotyped."

Many writers striving to write for children are indulgent aunts or grandparents who tell bedtime stories to their young kin and think that because they have held attention, whatever they tell to children surely will make salable manuscripts; it already has passed the acid test. Right here is where many writers make their first mistake—failure to understand the sophistication of youngsters. Children watch interesting, well-plotted stories on TV, and from the same source they may get more complete, more visual information than you can give them. Your storytelling is so appealing probably because the child listens in order to gain a few more minutes of attention before having to go to sleep. The older child may be more fascinated by your facial expressions and gestures than by what you have to tell him. Just try telling your tales when the child has a friend to play with or is engrossed in a new toy or hobby; if you can hold his attention in such circumstances, you are a storyteller!

Almost all editors of magazines for children and young people complain that the material they receive is trite. It is almost impossible that so many persons should have routine minds that can do no more than repeat the same old thing. Very likely the explanation is laziness rather than incompetency. Distrust the first idea that pops into your mind. If you thought of it so readily, almost certainly hundreds of other writers have also. If you really want to be a writer for children, read extensively in the field; read current children's magazines and books; read the classics; read back issues. Then you will have a background for judging whether what you plan to write is fresh or tired.

"Read good juvenile fiction," advises Doris B. Gold, editor of *The Young Judaean,* "in books preferably, and learn about content and vocabulary for the preschoolers, middle years and teen years. Carefully read stuff in magazines you've selected to send your stuff to. Learn to do research on at least a college level."

Stop, look, and listen, as the old railroad signs used to

say—or as James Langdon, editor of *Treasure Chest*, puts it: "Acquire and read at least *one* current issue of the magazine you intend submitting a manuscript to. For fiction, listen to how kids talk today—not for slang, but to learn their manner of expression. Few writers seem to know how kids really talk."

An encore comes from Dolly Debes, managing editor of *Golden Magazine for Boys & Girls*, who advises you to "study existing children's magazines and books, and don't write down to children. Remember that children do not enjoy hackneyed, corny stories any more than adults do."

Yet the desks of editors are loaded with stale accounts of the rabbit that would like to be a lion; the dog that behaves like a half-wit human instead of a normal animal; the flower that wants to please the little girl by showing its shining face long after the first severe frost.

The foregoing story themes and their ilk are sure bets for rejection slips, no matter how clearly they are told or how much "heart" goes into them.

Sure rejection-slip getters for teens are accounts of the hero's winning the game (football, basketball, baseball—are there no other sports?) just at the last minute. Or the unpopular girl, shunned because of the hand-me-down clothes she wears, who saves the rich girl from drowning and is beloved by all. There is no point in identifying more of this overripe material. Sufficient is the fact that 90 percent of the editors queried say that one of the most frequent reasons for rejecting manuscripts is that they are trite. "Platitudes and moralisms are no longer adequate for teenagers," says Bryan Woolley, editor of *Vision*.

Back of the outpouring of trite material, editors see other faults that lead to rejection slips. Fully one-third of all children's magazine editors suspect that many writers are merely impatient and careless, inclined to send in manuscripts that are poorly thought out, hastily written, and carelessly marketed. These are shortcomings that any normal person can overcome, but some editors bluntly state that what many authors write about is downright trivial, apparently stemming from minds incapable of saying anything meaningful!

To give the human mind some credit, it is doubtful that the requirements of most magazines are so elevated or so intellectual that they cannot be met by almost anyone equipped with normal intelligence and a fair command of English. Patience, perseverance, and perspicacity are the three Ps that virtually anyone can command; and they are the qualities needed for at least some measure of success in writing for children.

Essential to replacing rejection slips with checks is the knowledge of what editors want. Hardly any editor attempts to interest children of all ages; instead, periodicals are segmented to appeal to specific age groups from "tiny tots" all the way up to young adults. It would be futile to send a story about adolescent boys and girls to *Happy Times,* a magazine whose title does not clearly indicate its age direction, as do such other publications for small children as *Wee Wisdom* and *Nursery Days.* You can't always go by the title.

You might think that no writer would waste his time or money in sending a manuscript to a magazine without knowing at least to what age group it appeals. Any editor will tell you that every mail brings him material that is no more suitable for him than a beef sandwich is for a Hindu.

Editors are not rejection-slip happy; they rely on unsolicited free-lance manuscripts, and they want to buy them. Margaret S. Ward, editor of *Story World,* advises her contributors to "study several issues (4 to 6 at least) to get the general trend. Think in terms of the present-day child's interests—science, space, automation, speed—and write stories dealing with problems as they face them today." The editor of *Impact,* Curtis E. Johnson, concurs: "Become really acquainted with the present generation. Look beneath the surface to who they really are. Don't write to a generation that no longer exists."

A fairly frequent cause of rejections, according to Helen Decker, editor of *Happy Times,* is that "too many writers try to relive their own childhoods."

If such advice were heeded, editors would have greater respect for unsolicited free-lance manuscripts. At present this is not the case: 51 percent of all the editors find the "slush pile" of mixed value to them, and an astonishing 34 percent find it of little value! Only 15 percent find this source vital to them. Unless free-lancers realize what their markets want, editors will turn more and more to established authors—to the detriment of the free and easy access now afforded to the writer by the present method of submitting unsolicited manuscripts.

What are the magazines for children and young people like? Almost half of them are directed to youngsters under thirteen years of age. The next largest group is edited for young teens. Religious orders issue the majority of the magazines in this classification; the "books" are either rigidly denominational, interdenominational or nondenominational. Methodist orders publish 15 magazines; Baptists, 13; Lutherans, 15; and Catholics, 8. Fewer in number, but nonetheless fervid, are those issued by Mormons, Mennonites, United Brethren in Christ, Jews, and other groups, seemingly representing all sects (though there is no magazine for atheists). Only those that provide a market for free-lance manuscripts and are listed in market directories are referred to here.

Naturally, religious considerations largely determine the nature of the material used. For the most part, entertainment takes second place to furthering and interpreting principles of faith, setting a religious example, providing moral teaching, and inspiring the young reader.

These purposes do not have priority over inherent interest. "Do not moralize," warns Alice M. Evans, editor of *High School Signal, Guide for Juniors,* and *Sunday School Messenger.* "It is difficult to find stories for religious magazines containing the 'wonder' of childhood. Keep in mind the contemporary world in which the child lives and the faith to be communicated to him."

The secular magazines are not inimical to some of the purposes vital to the religious group, but their main "slant" is entertainment or education.

The preponderance of religious magazines is to the juvenile writer both a boon and a hazard. Probably you stand a somewhat better chance of selling to magazines of your faith than to a magazine of a different faith.

However, the writer who wants to specialize in this field will learn enough about the tenets of various religions to be able, as some free-lancers most certainly are, to write "across the board"—Protestant, Jewish, or Catholic. Editors don't ask to which faith you belong; they are interested only in how well you can write in harmony with the religion they represent.

Obviously, a Protestant denomination does not exactly duplicate some other division of Protestantism. The differences are of great importance to the editors of children's magazines, who control a viable instrument of indoctrination. A belief in God or Christ is common to all, but some sects have taboos—on girls' wearing lipstick and jewelry, on drinking coffee or tea, on fighting, dancing, or early dating, and quite a few more.

In recent years the children's magazines, religious and secular, have awakened to the challenge of the "now" generation. Spurred by the necessity to keep up with changing times, or lose influence or even the very existence of the magazine, editors (often egged on by business managers) give heed to what Robert M. Stalzer, president of Student Marketing Institute, said: "There is one exciting common denominator for young people from five to 25. That's their willingness to accept new ideas. . . . They're eager to spend money, and they have it to spend." An advertising firm points out that "teen spending now totals over 15 billion dollars a year. Teens also influence twice that amount in family purchases." Editors, no less than business managers, are impressed by such vast spending power.

Parents can afford to subscribe to magazines, and so can many teenagers; circulation figures are not diminishing. The market for manuscripts, therefore, will not decrease for years to come if ever. It has been pointed out that within a few years there will be more than twenty-seven million teenagers—a great potential readership. The demand for stories, articles, plays, poems, puzzles, games, and fillers shows no predictable let-up.

Editors of the juvenile magazines are very receptive to new writers, lamenting only the unevenness of unsolicited material. It is not editorial indifference that limits acceptances but the writers' own carelessness. Nevertheless, 70 percent of the editors, according to a survey made by the National Writers Club, buy half or more of their contents from "over the transom" submissions. Juvenile writers generally do not rely on literary agents, for the tithe of 10 percent taken by agents is simply not enough to interest them, since rates paid seldom amount to more than one to four cents a word. Established professional authors with high-paying markets for their work are hardly likely to be attracted to this field. This leaves a large market, consisting of some 150 magazines of all kinds and persuasions, open to the up-and-coming free-lance writer. This may not represent a "golden opportunity," but it is a steady and permanent source of sales and an area in which a writer may make his convictions strongly felt.

In the foregoing pages there has been mention of a change that has come about in the children's and young people's magazines—one that is real and sometimes even radical. "Face up to the changing times," the cry of George Grey, editor of *Big Beat,* is the watchword of most editors. No longer do they shy away from problems of racism, permissiveness, or early marriage; instead, they welcome contributions that meet the implied challenges in a manner harmonious with the purposes of their magazines. This new sophistication is indicated by the change of titles of one of the magazines issued by Parents' Magazine Press; born under the title of *Polly Pigtails*, it became *Calling All Girls;* its sophisticated readers now buy it as *Young Miss.*

Art must reflect the mores of the times. As one advertising firm points out, "Teenage girls mature earlier than ever. Today's teen girls are wearing lipstick starting at twelve years old, girdles before they are fifteen, and are donning seamless nylons and high heels several years younger than they once did." Just try telling them old wives' tales!

Almost as important as having something fresh and interesting to say is knowledge of your markets. Nothing exasperates an editor quite so much as inappropriate marketing of manuscripts. Editors take pride in their magazines, what they stand for and how they try to fulfill their functions. Make a friend of an editor by showing that you know the kind of magazine with which he is identified, and you'll have taken a big step toward getting a check.

Rev. Vernon D. Miller, editor of *Conquest, Challenge, Courage:* "Study the market and the position of the publisher regarding doctrine, church structure, and basic theological position. Be current in plot and characters, and do not 'baby' the reader. Be specific."

Dana Eynon, editor of *Junior Life:* "Study carefully the contents of the magazine to which you would like to contribute, and read all suggestions in any accompanying writer's guide prepared for that publication. This is time-worn advice, but still applicable."

Following are pointed comments from editors, which indicate exactly what they think is necessary for you to do in order to bypass rejection slips in favor of acceptances:

Write about what you know about

Brother Jason, C.F.X., associate editor of *Working for Boys:* "To be convincing, write about what you know most about. Use short but not choppy sentences; short paragraphs; action from the beginning; challenging plot or theme; masculine tone, even for girls."

Barbara Curie, elementary editor of *Weekly Bible Reader:* "Know the age group—their characteristics, their interests, what is within their understanding. Take every opportunity to observe children at school, at home, at play. Listen to their conversations and talk to them yourself."

Be a good craftsman

Alice Hershberger, editor of *Story Friends:* "Study your craft. Rewrite. Study and observe and interact with children. Listen to how they talk. Learn to feel *with* children. *Hear* your stories."

Gail Anderson, editor of *Junior Hi Challenge,* and *Senior Hi Challenge:* "Don't become bogged down at the beginning with introducing too many people, places and ideas. State the problem (preferably what young people might face today) and pack with teenage appeal and human interest."

Louis Schutter, editor of *Our Little Friend* and *Primary Treasure:* "*Show* instead of *tell.* Utilize scenes rather than a lot of narrative."

Thomas N. Hopper, editor of *Wee Wisdom:* "Short, simple, child-centered stories and projects, positive approach, are wanted. If each story puts across one idea that causes a child to see more in himself than he had glimpsed, we have accomplished our purpose."

Len Richardson, associate editor of *The National Future Farmer:* "Study a copy of the magazine, apply to nonfiction the same techniques that make fiction interesting, but remember that this group is sensitive to anything 'fakey.' Start by telling the reader 'why he should care' and then give him a character he can identify with, and a story that gives an insight into the life he leads."

Edna Rosky, editor of *In:* "Don't sound too authoritative in an article—rather, use a conversational approach and be up on teen language, fads, fancies and interests."

To improve the chance of acceptance of unsolicited free-lance manuscripts in the children's and young people's market, check these points:

1) Don't be in a hurry to submit your material. Read published stories and articles, to avoid repeating the familiar. Revise—many times, if necessary. Avoid the trite and the pointless. Check your manuscript with a discerning friend or professional critic.

2) Know as much as you can about a magazine before submitting material to it. Check market reports. Some editors prepare "tips for writers" sheets; ask for them. Most important, read the magazine (some editors will send a free sample copy).

3) Market intelligently. Indiscriminate marketing tends to alienate editors against unsolicited material and wastes your money, time, and hopes.

3

The Religious Magazine Market

"We buy from recognized agents only."

This statement, so discouraging to an aspiring writer (it is almost as difficult to interest a reliable agent as it is to find a purchaser of his manuscripts), is never heard among the religious magazines. Our recent survey, covering most of the publications in this field, revealed that not a single one of the editors *preferred* to buy from agents. More than half of them want to buy exclusively from writers directly, welcoming the "over the transom" submissions; only 27 percent would rather work with writers on assignment, and only 20 percent were neutral, showing no favoritism to manuscripts that come to them directly from writers or from agents.

How can you write for the religious magazines and gain something more than rejection slips? The answer is the same whether you are writing for the Protestant, Catholic, or Jewish periodicals: Do not violate the principles of the religious order that the magazine represents.

This does not necessarily mean a limited parochial

adherence to tenets, but required is a respect for religious ideas. What this may mean is illustrated by the example given by *Guideposts:* "Remember that *Guideposts* is an inspirational monthly magazine for all faiths in which men and women from all walks of life tell how they overcame obstacles, rose above failures, met sorrow, learned to conquer themselves, and became more effective people *through the direct application of the religious principles by which they live*" (italics added).

Adherence to this idea brings the first boost up the ladder to acceptances; next of importance is the necessity to realize that a religious tone is not of itself a *sine qua non*. Except for nondenominational publications, it is essential to understand something of the differentiating characteristics of various denominations. You can get yourself a quick rejection slip by not knowing that *The Baptist Leader* buys no manuscript that deals with liquor, tobacco, or obscenity; *Guide* will have nothing to do with theaters, dancing, or professional athletics; gambling and liquor are anathema to *Together*.

More than one-fourth of the editors queried said that a principal reason for rejecting unsolicited manuscripts is the writer's lack of an understanding of the religious tenets of their publications.

The fine distinction between magazines is illustrated by Mrs. Mary Pujolas, associate editor of *Canadian Messenger,* who says: "Do not think that an article which would suit a United States Catholic, Presbyterian or other religious publication would suit a Canadian periodical published by the same denomination."

The contemporary position of the religious magazines is emphasized by Helen Johnson, associate editor of *Together.* "Just to report what churches, or church people, are doing is not enough. It's necessary to know why, and this calls for some basic understanding of current theological thinking as well as background in the ecumenical discussions taking place today, and in the renewal movement. Changes are taking place rapidly today in religious attitudes, and the Church is making some valiant efforts to involve itself in the world. In interpreting all this, writers must understand the concept of the church as a community of believers."

To which Clayton C. Barbeau, managing editor of *The Catholic Viewpoint,* pertinently adds, "It is a mistake to think in terms of 'preaching' when thinking of a publication that is 'religious.' . . . We are not interested in articles 'slanted for the religious market' so much as in articles which are the result of the writer's real vision of what is going on in the Christian community and what is going on in the world and the relationship of the two."

The religious magazines do not treat subjects superficially any more than do the lay publications, according to Rachel Hartman, director of Editorial Development of *Christian Herald.* "Old subjects can be treated in a new way, but not in the same way as before. Many, many more subjects are religious or have religious implications than we used to think. We make less emphasis on the organized church, more on personal religion, than before."

About thirty different religious denominations are represented by 200 magazines. Can a writer cross boundary lines of faith and write for many or all? Only a third of the editors replied to this question in the negative: the others are convinced that a writer's own religion does not keep him from writing and selling across the board, provided that he understands the purposes and faith of the magazines for which he would write.

The negative side is represented by Wayne Christianson, executive editor of *Moody Monthly*. He maintains that "only writers within our own fundamentalist group can write with understanding and appreciation for our market. Few of those *within* this group know how to write for the reader or realize that the editor must make selections on the basis of what a given article will do for his readership."

Jack McCarthy, the amiable former executive editor of *Catholic Digest*, says that "a person doesn't have to be of the faith to write for Catholic publications. A goodly number of contributors are not Catholics. A goodly number, too, are real pros. What these pros do is exactly what the amateurs don't understand; that is, there are certain stories that are neutrals for the religious press."

Although the religious magazines encourage free-lance submissions, and at least 50 percent of the editors buy frequently from this source, no writer should be misled into thinking that this is a "pushover" market. "We find a common mistake of free-lancers is to think that the 'religious market' is an easy one, a last resort, or one which will accept shoddy sentimentality or mere pious platitudes," says Mr. Barbeau.

While religious magazines buy a great deal of material, it is bought for a purpose and with discrimination. The market today is not what it used to be, as many editors warn writers. In response to our questionnaire, editors defined the limits of this market so that free-lance writers can find a way to avoid the tortuous path of rejections.

"Avoid pious platitudes," is the number one guide-post offered by the Rev. Daniel Durken, O.S.B., editor of *Sisters Today.* "Let your manuscript say something of significance, let it say something original, and let it be stylistically acceptable. Write in a spirit of hope—we have enough of prophets of doom. And be thoroughly grounded in your topic through reading and personal experience."

"Don't preach," is the warning sigh of Albert P. Stauderman, associate editor of *The Lutheran.* "Sermons are meant to be heard, not read. Put yourself in the reader's place and talk to him as to a friend, avoiding stuffy, pious, platitudinous phraseology. Tell him something interesting that you've seen or heard or done."

Rhea Felknor, managing editor of *U.S. Catholic,* sadly admits that "Most of the manuscripts I see are dull, incompetent, one-dimensional treatments of a complex subject. . . . A writer should (1) not waste time on something that really isn't significant (some stories will be lousy no matter how much loving care is spent on them), and (2) really do his homework, i.e., *adequate* interviewing, research, etc." The Rev. M. J. Minster-man, managing editor of *Queen of All Hearts,* sums it up nicely by saying, "Use the head more than the heart."

When you have an eager market, it pays to prepare yourself to meet its requirements. Fifty editors report that in one year they bought 1,091 stories, 4,415 arti-cles, 902 poems, and 268 fillers. These sound like im-pressive numbers. However, they were bought from a total of 122,355 submissions! The 5 percent rate of acceptances nevertheless is greater than that of most of the other magazine groups.

The average number of manuscripts received by each religious magazine annually is about 1,500. Some have to cope with no more than 100 or less, though three periodicals received as many as 10,000 unsolicited manuscripts in a twelve-month period.

Naturally, because of space limitations, not all good manuscripts can be bought. Few writers can take comfort in this, for editors find that most of the material they reject has serious faults. Obviously, too many eager beavers do not heed Mrs. Pujolas' warning, "Do not use religious magazines to practice on!" If they did, it would not be necessary for fifty editors to complain that a major cause of rejecting manuscripts is that they are written in a dull and plodding manner. Make your writing "motivating, challenging, imaginative, and creative in approach," urges Fr. Augustine Hellstern, O.F.M., editor of *St. Joseph Seminary*.

Almost as many editors, forty-seven of them, find all too many manuscripts to be trite and uninteresting. "Research carefully so as to have something to say," Daniel Hertzler, editor of *Christian Living*, says. "Personalize, illustrate, so you will be read. Study the audience so they can be understood."

Yet another frequent reason for rejecting material is that it is poorly thought out. To avoid this, says Donald H. Gill, associate editor of *World Vision Magazine*, "familiarize yourself with the basics. Reach for subjects of genuine significance. Don't theorize without facts. Tell the story through selected situations, events, or other descriptive elements that make the point. Shape your approach and select your facts with your market in mind."

Most editors are disturbed by the fact that all too many writers mail out manuscripts blindly—a complaint voiced by editors of all types of magazines. Since many periodicals will send a free sample copy or a "statement of editorial policy," there is little excuse for a writer to fail to have some concept of the purpose and direction of a magazine. As Mr. McCarthy comments, "Basically, few writers understand the religious field and the reason is that none of them will take the trouble to look at the leading publications in the field. For the Catholic press, a writer can go to the rear of any Catholic church and find an array of practically all of the leading Catholic publications."

A way to make sure of what a magazine wants, says Wildon Colbaugh, editor of *Team,* is to "write to the magazine for editorial suggestions of current needs and ask for sample copies. A thorough understanding of the magazine's audience is needed. Writing for a specific publication will be more likely to produce a sale." Not imitation but an understanding of the publication is the purpose of study, so that you can "submit only those things to a given magazine," notes Nancy Hardesty, assistant editor of *Eternity,* "which you think are ideal for *it* in the light of what it generally publishes. In this way you can save your money and the magazine editor's patience."

"Everybody wants to preach," complains Jeremy Harrington, editor of *St. Anthony Messenger.* "Get the facts. Get us the striking, truly religious personalities. Do stories on interesting endeavors. Interview people who are doing things. If you just sit down at your typewriter and compose something, 99 chances out of 100 we will not be interested."

Space in any magazine presents problems. It behooves writers to be aware of and respectful of the stated word-count desired. Wordiness may earn a good article nothing more than a rejection slip. Howard E. Short, editor of *The Christian,* says, "We look for these qualities in the material we publish: Tight writing. Space is limited. We will accept an article of appropriate length in preference to one of better quality which requires cutting. We appreciate a candid, forthright approach, even on controversial subjects, more than attempts to cover up provocative statements with flowery language." To which Lucy R. Hoskins, editor of *Church Administration,* adds, "Say what you have to say concisely."

To represent the vast religious audience, the meaning and purpose of the religious press must be understood. In our survey, more than 35 percent of the editors rejected manuscripts because they showed a lack of an understanding of the tenets of the particular religious group to which they were submitted or because they lacked religious emphasis.

Representative and pertinent comments from several editorial points of view are these:

Frances Furlow, associate editor of *Presbyterian Survey:* "Avoid the veneer of religious terminology and deal with realities."

David F. Marshall, articles editor of *United Church Herald:* "Know the difference between depth and surface religion and faith. Any writer who can discover this difference (and it is sometimes quite radical) will be able to sell to the top-paying religious journals with

ease. An article on why there was an urban riot has
more religious significance than one on a historical religious leader or on current changing styles of worship.
The former has depth religion, the latter two are surface and almost impossible to sell to a high-paying religious market."

Alfred J. Gilliard, editor-in-chief of *The War Cry:*
"Avoid clichés, religious sentimentality, criticism of
other churches and their doctrines, use of out-of-date
illustrations or language now little understood; denun-
ciation, sadistic scolding of unbelievers. Exhibit gener-
osity, human kindness, understanding, compassion,
faith."

C. E. Page, managing editor of *The Congregation-
alist:* "The article must reveal a religion that makes
sense—and/or be a factual revelation of outstanding
tenets from world religions, revealing their persuasive
qualities in lives."

George H. Muedeking, editor of *Lutheran Standard:*
"In writing for Lutherans, be conscious of their theological presuppositions, since Lutherans are oriented
theologically."

A vital preliminary to an attempt to write for the
religious journals is the realization that religion itself is
changing. The old order passeth. This will be true for
some time to come, for the ecumenical spirit is a strong
wind blowing through the dusty convictions of the
past, and it will blow aside many nonessentials and out-
moded ideas. One editor states it this way: "Stress the
on-going changes that are occurring, and how these
changes reflect a new attitude toward one's personal

responsibility for his position and his service to others" (James F. Ryan, editor of *Catholic Market*).

Just because a magazine represents a religion, do not think that it must be soft or indulgent. This thought must be fairly prevalent to move Sister Mary Walter, editor of *The Magnificat,* to tell writers that they should "not praise your own manuscripts. Do not say, 'I need money.' Do not tell an editor what to do."

The writer who seriously prepares himself to write for the religious market should be widely read, not only in theology but also in other important areas. The necessity for this is the gist of what the Rev. Augustine P. Hennessy, editor of *The Sign,* means when he states his manuscript needs in this way: "We look for positive values in contemporary art, literature, politics, economics, science and technology. Articles should be written in popular, concrete and anecdotal style and contain nothing offensive to faith or morals."

Morality is in, but "forget the didactic approach," insists James F. Andrews, managing editor of *Ave Maria.* "Concentrate on in-depth reporting that clarifies causes. Broaden vision beyond what is normally considered religious. For example, we welcome articles on pollution, education, science, etc."

The foregoing comments illustrate the distance religious publications have come from the old-time "preachy," parochial magazines. This fact is underscored by the Rev. Jason Petosa, S.S.P., associate editor of *Catholic Home,* who asks you to "avoid simple-mindedness. Provide perspective, keep up with what's happening, and escape dullness. Interpret particular thought trends, events and practices in the Church today. Give practical information for readers to use in their family life."

A market that today buys fiction and verse as well as articles, a market that cherishes the free-lance writer and prefers to deal directly with him, is one to regard with respect. No longer are religious magazines to be thought of as a "last resort" for manuscripts rejected by the lay press. Your work has to be good to compete with the quality material editors now are buying.

This may not be a "beginner's market," but it is fully receptive to the aspiring writer who intelligently prepares himself to write for this extensive and prolific field.

4

The Literary Magazine Market

Most aspiring writers find the literary magazines a vast, uncharted field. Such strange names as *Pflugblatt, Entrails, Hanging Loose,* and *Clod & Pebble* abound. They have the reputation of paying nothing (at least in negotiable cash) or just a token amount. Consequently, some writers feel that almost anything is good enough for them. Like a skittish horse, some writers shy away from those publications whose contents are comprised mainly of strange, formless drawings, confusing poems, and stories with obscure or radical content.

Despite any distaste, the feeling persists that here is an easy market, a last resort where you may as well give away a manuscript that you can't sell. It is true that most of the literary magazines, except the august quarterlies, expect writers to be willing to be published without cash payment. However, it is equally true that new writers are welcomed more enthusiastically by literary magazines than by commercial magazines.

This does not mean that "just anything" will be accepted. Virtually all these publications have their pride, humble though the finished product may be. Nevertheless, the new writer has a better chance here to by-pass rejection slips, because competition generally is not great.

Competition comes largely from writers who are repeaters. Their natural habitat is the literary magazine, and the more far out it is the more consistently are they to be found securely within its pages. Eventually they succumb to the lure of the commercial press or they drop out of sight. The new writer is needed to fill the void.

Careless writing as an indication of the disrespect one may have for magazines that do not pay large sums will net a writer nothing but a rejection slip. "Writing must be an end in itself," says Richard Grossinger, co-editor of *Io*. "Those who try too hard to publish tend to pay more attention to the audience than to themselves and hence write trite things. Of 500 or more items submitted unsolicited, we have accepted two sets of poems. In both of these cases the persons had seen our magazine and thought their work relevant."

"Get off Cloud 9," advises John Snyder, publisher of *Gato*, "and turn out fewer sentimental pieces and turn that energy to developing a writing technique plus a realistic approach to the writing game, which requires accepting and integrating criticism sans the ego factor. Too many would-be writers are too thin-skinned when it comes to criticism—many have been defeated by it."

Thoroughness is the way to avoid many of the shortcomings that most of the editors found widespread in the unsolicited manuscripts sent them. H. Edwin O'Neal, editor of *Orion Magazine*, says that to avoid rejections, "It must be evident that the author has done some genuine research or thought intensely and personally about his subject. It is deplorable to receive articles full of fictional quotes, misapplied quotes and mistaken, false historical references. No matter how erudite the author, or deep his subject, the manuscript must be presented in sixth-grade language; his word pictures and analogues must be simple, direct and clear. He ought to leave his reader something to think about and to conclude for himself. Desire, very intensely, to say something meaningful and real that will, possibly, help another human being. Write all you possibly can. Do not write for money or for ego reasons. Those are side-effects that spoil most good writers, and to start by wanting the side-effects is to ruin possible talent. Write for the writing's sake. If you're good, you will have to fight the side-effects to remain good, to produce and to stay human."

Various editors are outspoken about the poor quality of material sent them, and, in effect, this is a warning to writers to be on their mettle and not to denigrate these publications.

A cardinal rule is to know the magazine for which you would write. "Writers ought at the very least to look at recent issues of whatever magazine they plan to submit to," says George Lanning, editor of *The Kenyon Review*. "If we've just done an article on a particular subject—theatre of the absurd, Faulkner, evil in the novel—we most emphatically won't be interested in another for a long time to come. Yet writers go on blithely submitting material that duplicates ground we've already covered. And if some took time to read our fiction, it seems unlikely we'd get quite so many stories about children, or the tons of stories with academic settings that pour down on our heads."

There is such a person as a devoté of literary magazines, just as there are those who watch every sports event on television. Richard R. Reynolds, editorial director of *Clod & Pebble,* advises: "Provide sophisticated material that will excite literary buffs."

Sage advice about what is expected of writers is given by the following four editors:

Constance Wagner, assistant editor of *Books Abroad,* expresses the "wish for a far greater respect among writers for the clarity and logic of the English word."

Winfred Blevins, editor of *A Nosegay in Black,* warns writers not to "regard us as a testing ground. Our poetry is of better quality than, say, *Harper's.* And our fiction is nearly as good as the poetry, though we have a little trouble competing here."

Dr. L. Smith Cranshaw, editor of *Just Thinking Magazine,* advises writers to "first of all, find out what the editor wants; 98 percent of the materials I receive must be returned because the writers did not ascertain my policy or needs."

Claire Emerson, editor and publisher of *Hoosier Challenger,* offers seven rules: "(1) Check your spelling! (2) Be neat with your typing. (3) *Never* send manuscripts without proper return envelopes and correct postage. (4) Follow the rules of the magazine you are submitting to—not some other one. (5) Please be tactful—editors are human. Avoid nasty notes to the editor (the worst writer will write the most nasty notes). (6) Don't send postal cards asking questions—without return envelopes and postage for all replies.

(7) Do study the format of any magazines submitted to —follow their rules. Don't expect long letters."

Considering the foregoing comments, it is not surprising that our survey showed that 70 percent of the editors believe that few would-be contributors seem to give any thought to the purpose of a magazine. As Ossie E. Tranbarger, American editor of *Phoenix Magazine,* says: "Aspire to write for literary magazines *only* if they are your preferred reading field."

To write for the really good magazines, preparation is essential. Paul Carter, editor of *The Colorado Quarterly,* advocates: "Read extensively, study writing and work at writing. Expect to do this for a considerable period before you send out any material, and then expect to continue the read-work-study routine perhaps for years before any material is accepted."

Obviously, too many would-be writers rush into marketing long before they have achieved a professional attitude. This motivated 65 percent of the editors queried to report that the quality of the average manuscript sent in by free-lance writers varies from fair to poor; only 35 percent rated it from rather good to very good (and only one editor voted for the latter). James Stephens, editor of *Cronopios,* was moved to say, "A good amount of the stuff received here is simply trash. It leads one to believe, as T. S. Eliot once noted somewhere, that the quality of intelligence of most 'writers' is not very high. In short, too much fakery is being sent out and even published by quite a few magazines."

Although only 30 percent of the literary magazines pay anything for accepted material (except in copies of the magazine or, occasionally, in prizes), there are definite benefits to being published in the better journals. A publisher may see a short story or article in a literary magazine that suggests to him the possibility of a book; he will seek out the writer and encourage him to expand the idea. Quite a few books have grown out of the fortunate combination of appearance in a small magazine and the alert ingenuity of a publisher.

As many as 30 percent of the editors of literary magazines recognize that their publications are a means of gaining wider recognition in other areas. Andrew E. Curry, editor of *dust*, says, "I ask the writer to use me as a 'sounding board' for where he wants or wishes to go."

About 25 percent of the editors look upon their publications as training grounds for new writers, but the majority, 42 percent, disdain "fringe benefits" and maintain that appearance in their magazines is an end and achievement of itself. Only three editors acknowledge that their books offer a comparatively easy way to get published!

The literary magazines range from the conservative to the extremely avant garde. Some are born to be short-lived, beating their feeble wings for an issue or two and then no more. Others, like *Hudson Review, Prairie Schooner,* and *Partisan Review,* have exhibited a longevity comparable to that of the commercial magazines. Twenty-three of the literary magazines have been given a shot in the arm through grants by the Coordinating Council of Literary Magazines, totalling more than $75,000. The rest must depend upon big-hearted donors and a modest number of subscribers. Very few accept (read: can get) advertising.

Writers do not fool literary editors by sending poor manuscripts, even though on occasion the magazines fail to print better material. A cross section of the editors finds almost all of them commenting on the poor quality of material received. Forty editors decried the lack of originality; thirty-five found the writing dull and stodgy; twenty-eight found little in the manuscripts worth saying, and when an idea was present, it was poorly developed.

Comments Norman Moser, editor of *Illuminations:* "A great many young writers are content to display overworked or personal ideas or feelings which haven't been elevated into solid renditions of experience, which is what writing is. Not enough attention is given to details. An experience in art must somehow seem unusual or unique even when it deals with a commonplace type of situation or theme. Lots of writers feel that personal sincerity is enough."

Whatever their convictions regarding the function of their periodicals, most of the editors will go well out of their way to try to help promising free-lance writers, a form of editorial collaboration rarely found in any other market area. A cross section of the literary magazines reveals that forty-four editors write a personal letter of rejection when a manuscript shows promise; thirty-two tell why a piece of work was rejected; and twenty-seven suggest revisions that might make the manuscript acceptable.

The constructive attitude of so many of the editorial staffs is reflected in the following comments:

Thomas A. Stewart, president of *The Harvard Advocate:* "(1) Don't be afraid to submit material. (2)

Don't be discouraged by rejections. (3) Ask for advice and help in improving your writing—editors *are* people."

Thomas McEvilley, editor of *Mt. Adams Review:* "Be unembarrassed about your work; put *anything* in it that pleases you."

James Koller, publisher and editor of *Coyote's Journal:* "Do not write *for* anybody. Write what you have to. A careful examination of the work similar to your own (in published form) will turn up potential markets."

Jules Chametzky, co-editor of *Massachusetts Review:* "Don't try to do what everyone else is doing, but don't be surprised that editors reject good pieces because they have a tone or idea in mind—an editorial 'idea' about the kind of magazine they want."

James Bruce Anderson, editor of *What Can This Charlatan Be Trying To Say:* "Dare to be uniquely unique. Dare to be uniquely traditional. In ideas, know the field, then break new ground."

Norma Almquist, editor of *Ante:* "Be absolutely honest to your own vision. Revise and revise until every scrap of deadwood, cliché, phoniness, sentimentality, is destroyed at every level—language, plot, motivation, etc."

P. E. Johnston, editor and publisher of *Dasein: The Quarterly Review:* "Spend more time writing and learning how to write than in submitting to publications. Learn the basic mechanics of syntax of English before attempting to be *original*. Absorb your culture and spend more time listening and observing than in talking. Spend little time with other so-called writers and more with people. Spend time with people in the other arts, and try to find out what they are doing and how it can affect writing as an art. Most of all, read, read, and read! Once you learn the trade, be confident in your own abilities because editors are not infallible. Do not regard a rejection slip as anything other than a piece of paper issued on a certain date."

Joseph North, editor of *American Dialog:* "Study writers you like. Write a lot, rewrite, polish, do not go solely on native ability. Hemingway told me he often rewrote a short story 20 to 25 times. Most good writing is in the rewrite. In brief, sweat it out."

Some 250 literary magazines are reported in *Writer's Market,* published by *Writer's Digest.* This is a fair representation of the total number of these publications, though it is by no means inclusive. The type of material that dominates the tables of content is poetry, used by 242 of them. Articles are used by 175 of these magazines; fiction by 152; criticisms by 106; satire by 62; plays by 9; and essays by only 7. Only 41 of the 250 magazines pay for material.

The literary magazines represent a potential market for more types of material than do other groups. However, the magazines range from the shoddy to the highly discriminating. What your writing means to you in terms of craftsmanship, integrity, and creativity will dictate the kind of magazine you will seek.

Just what some of these magazines may mean to you is implicit in the statement of William Farris, editor of *Sunburst:* "The object of the literary magazine is to offer a showplace to the poet of today, to assist in his development, and to assure him a reliable listening post when he speaks."

5

The Trade Journal Market

What a window display! The manikins are so lifelike that one is reminded of the John Collier story about department-store dummies that come to life at night after everyone has left the store. Now this is something for a trade journal, because obviously it is getting much attention. Home and to the typewriter to get impressions down while they're fresh and compelling. Then off with the manuscript to a business journal. It ought to be a sale.

There are approximately 2,000 trade journals in the United States, ranging all the way from the *Journal of Recreational Mathematics* and *Journal of Typographical Research* to such prosaic titles as *Meat Magazine,* and *Corset and Underwear Review.* Approximately 1,000 of these magazines are actively in the market for articles. In no other category are there so many potential buyers from which to choose!

What about the panegyric written by the window-gazer? If he has any knowledge of the diversity of trade papers, he will know at least enough to send his article to a magazine directed to dry goods or dress merchants, or perhaps to a manufacturer of manikins. Will it sell? No matter how poetic or appreciative his piece may be, it is foredoomed to a rejection. Not only will it be sent back, but the editor will groan once more with dismay and wonder if it's worth while to pay any attention to "over the transom" manuscripts.

Robert R. Jones, managing editor of Agricultural Publishers, insists, "Get more *facts*. Get the real story below the surface; know what your editor needs and work closely with him. Don't try to substitute flowery writing for substance in your copy."

The trade paper writer is essentially a reporter, not an essayist. As Walter Kubilius, editor of *Printing Impressions*, effectively states: "The most common problem is the assumption that *words* are more important than *facts*. Too many writers feel that vague generalities that fill space would be of interest or value to anyone. Don't write unless you can actually tell somebody something that he does not already know. Anybody can write—but it takes skill and brains to provide information. A true writer deals not with words, but with ideas, facts, and emotions."

Is our window-gazer discouraged because his manuscript was rejected? He shouldn't be. In no other commercial market group will he find editors so eager to work with him, to point out his shortcomings, to revise his copy, and to pay for it. Writing skill is a secondary consideration, so an inexperienced but intelligent writer can serve his apprenticeship here and even earn some money while doing so. The noted novelist, William E. Barrett, author of *Lilies of the Field* and other books, began his career as a writer for trade papers, and so have many other successful writers.

The willingness of editors to work with fledgling authors is clearly stated by Gene Bennett, editor of *Candy Industry & Confectioners Journal:* "I have gone out of my way to guide writers, since they were initially unfamiliar with our field and its needs, etc. However, here is the decision a writer must make: Is it worth his time to develop a field? I for one am willing to work with a free-lancer, given the chance."

"Few editors will return a manuscript that obviously reflects an eager desire by the new writer to 'get into the scope of the magazine,'" says Robert M. Brown, editor of *Communications Equipment Marketing.* "Trade magazines can use alert, observant people who can write, even though the writers themselves may not be 'experts' in that particular field. . . . It's those who take one look at a trade magazine listing, size up the page rates, and ship off an article on 'How to Sell Better' that irk me particularly. Write the editor, ask for his suggestions, and—by all means—get a few back issues in front of you!"

Willing as many trade journal editors are to work with new writers, there are limits. Leo F. Spector, editor of *Assembly Engineering,* makes no bones about it. He writes as follows: "My feeling is that free-lancers generally fail in writing for the technical press because they bite off more than they can chew. Good writing is often not as important to us as a good subject (one that relates to our audience), treated in a meaningful way and presented in the 'language' of our audience. Some of the submissions—in fact, most of the submissions we get—are ridiculous. They show a complete lack of understanding of our audience and the subjects we deal with. Our time is valuable, too, and after we go so far with a writer who shows apparently no attempt to understand us, we give up."

Our window-gazer could have spared himself a rejection slip and the editor's exasperation had he taken the time to understand why trade journals are different from other magazines. He would have known that people in industry, manufacturing, and various trades subscribe to appropriate periodicals to learn how to conduct their enterprise more efficiently or with greater profit. When they want entertainment or news they turn to *Playboy* or *Newsweek*.

Herbert Saal, editor of *American Dairy Review*, puts it bluntly: "Readers of any trade or business magazine are interested only in how to make money in their business. This is the kind of article they want to see. The greatest need in this field is for 'how-to' stories, exemplified by specific instances of how a problem was overcome."

Similar advice is offered by Leo E. Oberschmidt, managing editor of *Brick & Clay Record:* "Try to follow *very closely* in the niche of the magazine, the audience to which the editorial policy is aimed. General articles which fit many fields by changing a few words are of little value and can be written by almost any college graduate who has taken a course in some form of journalism."

Our window-gazer was not necessarily at fault in his choice of subject, for it has salable possibilities. What interested him could have interested an appropriate trade paper if he had understood better what such a publication wants. He could have obtained an interview with the manager of the store or with the window trimmer to learn who had originated the window display, what the cost was to set it up, how it helped business and to what extent, and how profitable it was from an economic or public relations standpoint. The article could have indicated also how other merchants might adapt a similar display in connection with their business.

He should know that an esthetic appreciation of the window display, no matter how poetic it is, will never find its way into print in a trade paper. He should know how to avoid the failure of many unskilled writers "to recognize that stories such as case histories are published to help the reader to operate and profit from a better business," according to Nathaniel Holmes II, editor of *Coin Launderer & Cleaner,* who adds, "Vital statistics do not help—but what the businessman does to improve and why he does it, is what makes the story *helpful* to the reader of the trade journal."

It is essential that writers understand the slant of any trade paper. How you may do this is told by Edward H. Ellison, editor of *Fence Industry Trade News,* in this way: "Place yourself in the position of a dealer who reads the publication. Don't puff any article with superlatives to create lineage. We only delete and rewrite. The dealer wants to know about products, people in the field, how they operate, whether successful profit-wise, how they go about making sales, what equipment is used, how employees are treated to produce the best results. Trade material has to be slanted to the trade, not to the consumer."

Our survey of the trade journal field shows that 69 percent of the editors queried are eager to work with

promising new writers who show a genuine willingness
to learn. Just demonstrate to an editor that you are
serious about writing for his publication, that you did
some advance reading of his magazine and about the
business he represents, and that you have a modicum of
intelligence to back up your ambition—and you are in.

Don't be one of the would-be writers from whom 45
percent of the editors cringe as they read the daily mail.
In it they find manuscripts totally unsuited to their
publications. You can see how they feel. You cannot
blame Chris Anastos, editor of *The Milk Dealer* and
The Ice Cream Review, for saying, "General articles
distributed in a scattershot approach are unneeded and
unwanted. We want and can use articles that show
knowledge of our industries and that provide useful information to our readers. In other words, the articles
must be completely specific, original (clippings and
canned releases are available to us, too), and provide
help that can't be obtained elsewhere." A figure of
speech sometimes helps impress this point more forcefully; Otto J. Scott, editor of *Rubber World,* says, "We
do not need shotguns, but well-aimed rifles."

Querying the editor before you put in too much time
on your piece is a wise and often essential procedure.
The editor wants to know that you have an intelligent
concept of the purpose of his magazine before he en-
courages you. On your part, you want to know if your
planned subject has been covered recently by the magazine, what special slant the editor might want, and the
approximate number of words he can use.

This is clearly spelled out by Earl Seaton, editor of
Oil and Gas Equipment: "Study articles in a magazine
to see what the editor's needs are. Then, if you're inter-

ested in writing for him, tell him. Send him a sample of your published material. Ask for the details on his needs—if you have studied his magazine first. If you haven't seen his magazine, tell him your business and ask for a copy."

Another reason for reading a publication first, according to Lester Nafzger, associate editor of *Maintenance Supplies* and *Contract Cleaning,* is that "there are a number of taboos in our field which must be known. Please request copies of our magazines before attempting to write for us."

The importance of a query is illustrated by this example given by Mel Hosansky, editor of *Photo Dealer:* "I have received some 30 or 40 articles from a single writer on subjects that never appear in our magazine. I suppose the only piece of advice that I consider of major importance is that free-lancers find out what we want before sending material."

A query can be a time saver. "Make sure you know exactly what the editor wants before beginning an assignment," says Paul T. Knapp, editor of *Display World.* "This will save time and enable the writer to get all the information in the first interview."

What should you put into a query letter? "Send enough information in a letter of inquiry," advises Robert B. Konikow, editor of *Advertising & Sales Promotion,* "to permit me to make judgment." It is always well to say also what you know about the industry represented by the editor's magazine, what your writing experience is, and how great your ability to carry through an assignment is.

Some aspiring trade paper writers look about their community and note that certain factories or unusual industries are located there. This is one first step toward salability of an article, though it is not enough merely to recognize the existence of story-pregnant subjects. "Stick to writing about things you understand," says W. G. Gude, editor of *Foundry*.

"Don't profess expert knowledge in fields where you have only superficial acquaintance with the subject," is the warning of Dorothy Eudy, editor of *Non-Foods Merchandising* and *Convenience Store Journal*, and she is backed up by Helen Emerson, managing editor of *Hospital Management*, who finds that "usually what is submitted is pretty routine and is usually a rehash of something read in another publication, which article may not have been very well done to begin with!"

There is no use trying to get away with something, for editors can recognize a borrowed source, whatever it may be. The best way to earn a rejection slip and at the same time alienate the editor you are trying to please is to rely solely on a newspaper clipping or a publicity handout. Listen to R. F. Crawford, editor of *Electric Heating Journal:* "Today I received from a free-lancer a story borrowed almost word-for-word from a news release distributed by a public relations agency. I consider this practice grossly unethical."

The willingness of trade journal editors to help writers is demonstrated by their freely offered advice to those who aspire to success in this field. Brandon F. Timm, associate editor of Allied Publications, issuing more than a half dozen magazines, is explicit: "Research your subject thoroughly before submitting articles, and get a reputation with a publisher as a writer who knows *exactly* what she or he is writing about, an author who can be depended upon to submit factual, accurate articles, without error. Avoid editorializing, such as calling the French Revolution 'tragic,' all Germans 'militarists,' pre-Christians or non-Christians 'pagans,' and the like. Write objectively, without interjecting personal likes or dislikes or assuming that your reader will agree with your adjectives."

Here are five suggestions that, if followed, can help to make you a successful trade paper writer:

V. A. Kehoe, associate editor of *Domestic Engineering:* "Work from an outline for all technical material. Write a decent lead."

Marvin Wilder, editor of *Casual Living* and *Juvenile Merchandising:* "Find an angle. Don't ramble—say it and be done. Organize your work so that it doesn't have to be completely rewritten. Recognize a lead when you have one."

Sidney Fineman, managing editor of *Graphic Arts Monthly:* "Write specifically for our market; avoid generalities. Dig deeper; most of what we get is superficial."

Hugo G. Autz, editor of *The Sporting Goods Dealer:* "Get to the point and hold down copy. A few hundred words and one or two photos will sell easier than 1,200 words and six photos. Don't worry so much about payment or rates. Write, submit, and they will take care of themselves."

Neal Pronek, editor of *Pet Industry:* "Submit a professional-looking manuscript, clear and free of mistakes that result from downright carelessness. Know what you're talking about. Make sure that photos are pertinent to the body of an article, not just general themes that have no editorial value."

The need for professionalism is perhaps more important in this area than in any other magazine group. All its readers in a sense are experts in a particular field, and therefore are quick to recognize anything phony or inaccurate. As editors point out, writers must be specific and sure of their facts.

Ben Marsh, editorial director of Ojibway Press (publishers of eighteen magazines), urges writers to "ask questions, be thorough and specific, not general. Check your copy with the subject. Write with skill and style."

Know your limitations. "Some writers tackle complicated subjects in which they are not qualified," says Walter W. Balcerak, associate editor of *Supermarket Merchandising* and *The Discount Merchandiser*. "We have neither the time nor a large enough staff to check his 'facts.' Here's what we like: (1) easy-to-read, personalized writing; (2) an explanation of how a specific operator was able to increase his sales or profit, or reduce his costs; (3) specific facts to back up statements, with figures and photos if possible."

Trade paper editors want to give assignments to a writer on whom they can depend; this is a boon to the conscientious writer. Rules to follow when writing on assignment are offered by two editors:

James P. Hamilton, managing editor of *Motor Age:* "(1) Inquire first; (2) be willing to write on speculation—at least at first; (3) send twice as many facts as we can use—and make sure you remember you're writing a business article, not a consumer article; (4) deliver on time, and (5) learn how to take decent photographs."

John F. Berry, managing editor of *Canner/Packer:* "When you receive a request to write a story in your area, check it out right away and let us know if you can—and are willing—to do it. Don't expect future assignments if you are tardy in answering our inquiry."

The trade-journal writer today is armed with a note pad and a camera. The interview with a key person is the follow-up to the idea for a story. Then comes the picture. It is as important to know how to get a picture, taken by yourself or by a photographer, as it is to write the story. "The number of writers with cameras has increased," observes Mel Hosansky of *Photo Dealer*. "I wish, however, that the number with cameras who know how to use them had increased also. Good pictures are rarer than they ought to be."

What should a good picture be? H. F. Forhan, editor of *Auto Laundry News*, explains: "Good glossies are those directly connected with the slant or slants featured in the article, always with people in the pix when possible." And Glenn S. Hensley, editor of *Farm & Power Equipment*, adds: "Too many writers submit old-fashioned, stand-em-up-and-shoot pictures. These do not supplement the story in any way."

Not every magazine in this area has a "welcome new writer" sign hanging out. Indeed, A. Manola, editor of *NAHB Journal of House Building*, is sure that "trade magazines are not a profitable market for free-lance writers." Another editor, Hartley W. Barclay, managing editor of *Automotive Industries*, shares this view when he says, "In the field of business writing, we do not encourage free-lance writers. The best move to success is to find a position on an established magazine and learn the field, and get a reputation."

Paul V. Farrell, editor of *Purchasing Magazine*, avers that he "would rather spend money to send one of our own staff to cover a story than to put the time and effort into training a free-lancer to get the material we need and to write it our way."

Fortunately, these views are merely the slender finger of shadow on a sunny day, for almost all editors in this area are eager to work with free-lance writers and to help them if necessary.

The easiest access to sales is via the magazines that pay low rates; their editors try to make up in cooperation what they cannot give in money. Payment among the trade journals varies from 1¢ to 8¢ a word, from a flat payment of $10 for an article, to $250. A few magazines pay space rates, based upon the column length of a printed article rather than on the word count.

Almost all the magazines pay extra for photos, ranging from $1.65 a picture to $7.50 or more.

There are somewhat more magazines that pay on publication than those that pay promptly on acceptance. Some editors maintain that they cannot know how much of a story will be used until it is set up in type and printed in an issue of the magazine; hence the necessity to pay on publication.

Based on reports by editors, these are the types of articles wanted most by trade journals: good case histories; useful ideas; technical step-by-step stories; news of activities; interview-type articles; survey-type reports; merchandising and management stories; features on new ideas; features on dealers using some *one* unusual technique to increase the success of their business; in-depth articles on the principles, selection, and application of equipment; how-to-do-it types; success profiles; merchandising photos and captions.

Perhaps those aspiring writers who look for an easy way to make sales should be warned that in this time of widespread experience and mounting competition, there is no way so easy that good craftsmanship can be ignored.

"Good writing is the hardest work in the world," says Jack Hobbs, managing editor of *Electronic Technician*. "No writer is any good who does not know his subject thoroughly nor how to write about it in the fewest and simplest possible words. Technical jargon, cliches, and hackneyed phrases take up from 15 percent to 25 percent of today's technical writing—to say nothing of plain redundancy. My advice is for writers to learn how to write."

6

The Greeting Card Market

Perhaps no writer of greeting card material makes a living from this type of work alone unless he has a regular job with a greeting card company. However, a good many writers do make at least occasional sales.

Edward Hohman tells in *The Writer* that he started out with no particular knowledge of what greeting card companies want and at first reaped nothing but rejection slips. He stuck with it, learning as he wrote, and sold $1,000 worth of material to them within a fairly short period of time. This isn't bad for a part-time fling at a market!

The greeting card companies offer one of the easier markets because they are usually wide open to material. What they want must be very short; a writer must give a great deal of attention to his idea, polishing it until it really stands a chance of acceptance.

This market has grown to gigantic proportions. In 1965 some 200 greeting card companies sold $800 million worth of cards, representing a total of new cards that year in the amount of 200 million.

Hallmark Cards, the leader of them all, has 40,000 outlets in 75 countries, employing 800 sales representatives to sell the average yearly output of 12,000 newly designed cards.

Only about 35 publishers are actively in the market for material, according to the listings in writers' magazines. However, this number includes the Big Five— Hallmark, Norcross, Gibson, Rust Craft, and American Greetings—that virtually dominate the market. A survey conducted by the National Writers Club reveals that 70 percent of all the companies actively in the market for material buy frequently from unsolicited submissions. Hardly any other market can equal this respect for the "slush pile."

Most editors are in the market for contemporary or studio type of cards, with a demand for seasonal ideas running second. A lively interest is shown also in novelty, special occasion, humorous, children's, sophisticated, and religious cards. The offbeat commands little attention.

Editors want to encourage free-lance writers who show any inclination to be thorough and professional. "Study cards on the market," suggests Carolyn Clapp, editor of Little Eve Editions. "Know the type of card the publisher prints before submitting anything."

"Study our cards on the rack for the type of material we use," advises Ed Hartman, creative director of American Colortype Co.

John W. Rehner, editorial director of American Greetings, offers a good working method: "For rhyming verse, first write down your idea in prose, then, keeping the same idea, set it to rhyme. *Don't* rhyme for rhyme's sake! Proofread your material before sending it in."

"Be different, be unusual, and don't be afraid to be yourself," is the summation of Ruth Fishel, owner of Keep 'n Touch.

The prevalence of shortcomings in prose and verse that stigmatizes much of the unsolicited material causes editors to lament the trite ideas, poor writing, unsatisfactory rhyme and rhythm, and the too-close patterning on existing material. The following suggestions of editors, if followed by writers, will increase the rapport between them. Kent DeVore, managing editor of Hallmark Cards, tells you that "ideas may be submitted in any number of formats, from typed cards to fully illustrated roughs. However, it is essential that the writer's name and address be on the back of each idea, and a stamped, self-addressed envelope be included. Ideas must be based on a strong and very humorous switch or gagline or a very sendable compliment or wish. Avoid insulting, sarcastic, off-color or distasteful ideas."

Some editors are specific about the way they want material submitted. Helen Farries, editor of Buzza-Cardozo, wants you to "put each verse or sentiment on a small, separate piece of paper about 3 x 5 inches, with name and address on each, and enclose a stamped, self-addressed envelope for return. Don't send more than a dozen at a time and don't 'swamp the editor' with many examples at one time. Be sincere, conversational and leave out limiting factors. Research card shops—it's wonderful training."

George F. Stanley, Jr., editor of Vagabond Creations, prefers ideas to be typed on paper that is 2 x 3 inches.

"Make the presentation in typed form, easy to read, easy to return. Be sure to make your copy short and about everyday items with a clever *surprise* in the punch line."

Send at least five ideas at one time if you want to please Carolyn Clapp. "Don't bother with elaborate art work if you want only to sell the copy," she says.

Additional sound advice is offered by these editors:

Stella Bright, verse editor of Sangamon Co.: "Please be sincere. Keep your verse easy to read, using words we usually find in everyday speech. Keep it suitable for more than one person."

Ed Letwenko, art director of United Card Co.: "Studio card captions should not be lengthy. Keep them short and sweet with a punch line. Make them almost like a one-liner."

F. Vercoe, publisher of Curtis Contemporary Cards: "Ask each publisher for his market letter before submitting the material, and save a lot of time for everybody —and also increase your chance for sales."

Margaret Gould, editor of the general line of Gibson Greeting Card Company: "Don't be poetic. Think of greeting cards as notes which carry a wish, a compliment, or an expression of appreciation. After writing a verse, analyze it for meter, rhyme and content. Does it exactly convey your thought? Would most of the people you know be likely to send it? Remember that many thousands of potential customers may read the verse you write, so make it sendable and receivable by all."

Dolores Anderson, editor-in-chief of Rust Craft: "Read greeting cards in the stands and become very familiar with all kinds, all companies. But *don't copy* what you see in the stores (with a word or two changed) and send it to greeting card companies as your original work."

Any writer who aspires to write for the greeting card companies will find the sage instruction of H. Joseph Chadwick, editor of Barker Greeting Card Company, inspiring and practical: "Study—study—study the greeting card business until it comes out of your ears. This means to read every greeting card you can find and every book there is on writing greeting cards. And once you write an idea and believe it is good, don't give up on it. Keep submitting it until you run out of markets. Then put it away for about a year, and start it through the markets again. Remember the old saying: the only difference between an amateur and a professional is that the amateur gave up!"

7

The Confession Story Magazine Market

A friend of mine told me that one evening she had a visitor, a budding writer like herself. Indiscreetly, she told the girl of a true incident to test if it were interesting. It must have been more interesting than my friend imagined, for the girl promptly wrote a story around it and sold it to a confession magazine. Nonplussed, my friend wrote it up also—and sold her version to the same magazine!

That happened some time ago. Today the confessions are not so repetitious. You can't get away with anything of that sort now. Another writer who had collaborated with a friend in writing confessions broke up the partnership. Unknown to the other, each sent virtually the same story on which they had been working to the same magazine. The editor told both writers that she would never read another manuscript by either.

The market for confession stories is wide open. Editors are most cooperative with those who show any understanding of what is wanted for their magazines.

What about the familiar formula, "Sin, Suffer, and

Repent"? Proceed cautiously if you follow it. Otherwise, most likely you will fall into the error of using trite situations and unreal characterizations. People do not fit into a formula—even in confession stories. Today these magazines deal with reality, publishing stories in which sin is no more prominent than it is in your neighborhood. However, 75 percent of the editors say that a *confession* angle is essential in their stories. The other 25 percent are not so insistent. Keep in mind that it is the "confessing" part that distinguishes most stories in this area rather than telling the story in the first person.

The attitude of the confessions today is revealed in a trade-paper advertisement of *True Story* which reads as follows: "The problems of unwed mothers, divorce, alcoholism, and interracial marriage aren't fairy tales. . . . Readers learn about life through the experience of others. And also look to us for guidance."

Ruth Beck, editor of *Real Confessions* and *Modern Love Stories*, wrote me that "we look for credibility of plot, real-life situations, authentic backgrounds, accuracy of medical details or other technical material.

"The story told by a female narrator which has a happy or upbeat ending is most likely to succeed with us. The narrator should be a likable person who may have some weakness in her character that leads to her difficulty. Tell her story in simple language, colloquial rather than dramatic style. Plenty of action in the plot, plenty of dialogue—are what we look for.

"Stories written today should reflect our modern scene. Too many of the stories we receive could have been written in the 1920's and in the depression years of the 30's. The writer should deal with those aspects of life which are a vital part of the current scene."

Most editors like a man-woman sex angle in their stories, but only one out of the entire field favored an overt sex situation. The "facts of life" simply are not ignored. As *True Story* says in its advertising, "Parents are finally telling their kids where babies come from. Because today if you don't tell somebody the truth they'll find it out the hard way. Mother Goose isn't much help to an unwed mother."

All the confession magazines are geared to young married people; only half of them appeal equally to teenagers.

Confession stories are supposed to be true, as the titles of so many magazines indicate, but in most cases only a basis in truth will suffice. As Hellen Fain, editor of *Intimate Story* and *Your Romance,* advises, "Follow the tabloids for current situations."

A key to the source of women's problems was presented by John Mack Carter, editor and publisher of *Ladies' Home Journal,* who spoke at a conference of the Electrical Women's Roundtable. "It's easy to say to women," he said, " 'you've never had it so good,' but with more improvements comes greater discontent because of greater expectations and more needs to satisfy."

At the same meeting Virginia Van Nostrand of the Whirlpool Company, said that "with women's new freedoms she now is eager to be more daring and to explore; to enjoy life and leisure; to be more creative and to dominate."

These ambitions will give rise to new problems. Such current problems are the stuff of which confession stories are made.

Bruce Elliott, editor of *True Love,* defines the term "confession story," as follows: "It's a believable story told in the first person—sometimes reflecting the ordinary emotional conflicts of ordinary people, sometimes reflecting the extraordinary emotional conflicts of ordinary people. A confession story should emerge as a fresh, vital human document that not only delivers a punch but . . . also involves the sympathies of the reader. Whether it is a story of raising children or raising Cain, the narrator must keep reader sympathy— even in the face of wrongdoing. By the time the story reaches its conclusion, the reader must know something about her own frailties and the frailties of others.

"Not all confessions are stories of what people have done and wished they hadn't, or stories of what people have not done and wished they had. The main purpose of many a confession story is to inspire the reader to hope. Sources for confession plots are all around you. Tap those sources, whether they be the experience of your parents, your relatives, your friends, or yourself. In this you must be ruthless. No writer can afford the luxury of not using his most intimate world for his writing."

Henry P. Malmgreen, editor of *Modern Romances*, gives this version of what a confession story is: "A confession. The narrator has to have something to confess —something to blame herself for. And the events of the story—particularly its climax—must flow naturally and inevitably out of that original blameworthy act. . . . A story that isn't a confession is almost certain to be a story without a theme—that is, a story which points no moral, teaches the narrator (and by extension the reader) no lesson."

The editorial search for something fresh is endless. Ruth Beck, editor of *Real Confessions* and *Modern*

Love Stories, is concerned. She urges writers to "look for timely themes. Avoid repeating the same old hackneyed plots and situations. Editors can't fill an issue with stories in which every narrator's troubles begin with drunken parents or with a set of parents killed in a car accident. Horrible as highway accident statistics are, there are more people killed in confession magazines than populate our over-populated world. A little more effort, and the writer can surely create a different set of circumstances which will bring our heroine to woe."

A way to find this difference is suggested by Florence V. Brown, editor of *True Life Confessions, True Romantic Confessions,* and *Secret True Confessions,* when she suggests that you "read enough published confessions so that you will avoid using the same stereotyped plots and characterizations. Any time we find a really original plot, a believable and well-written story, we are anxious to buy it."

The only way to redeem a trite situation, points out Jean Sharbel, editor of *Secrets, Revealing Romances, Daring Romances,* and *Exciting Confessions,* is to "add a fresh angle."

The confessions is no place for the Gothic, the macabre, or the tragic; an unhappy ending is eschewed by most editors, though Ariel Strong, editor of *Tan,* reports that for her, "stories need not have a happy ending, but they should show some definite conclusion or realization on the part of the author."

Shunned is the unsympathetic central character or narrator. Florence J. Moriarty, editor of *True Confessions,* is definite about this. "We are not interested in narrators who are unsympathetic. Readers find it impossible to relate to them."

Appraisal of a confession magazine, as part of your marketing plan, is recommended by Frank Gould, editor of *True Romance* and *True Experience*. "Try to understand us," he urges in an article he wrote for *The Writer's Yearbook*. "We're not going high-hat. We're not seeking literary masterpieces. To the best of our ability we simply want to be what we are. We wish to print true stories; they need not be confessions, they need not be sordid, they need not be hackneyed. But they need to be efforts on your part, and on our part, to write and print the best true stories of our times. They can and should be good stories about love, about family life, about health, religion, the rebellion of youth and the problems of parents. There is no limit to true stories."

In many stories strong emotional appeal is the key to acceptances. "Start out with a good scene," is the suggestion of Ardis Sandel, editor of *Real Story, Real Romances, Uncensored Confessions,* and *My Love Secret Confession.* "Think of your characters as real people in sexual and emotional situations."

The common complaint of editors is that writers are unfamiliar with their special slant, the policy that differentiates their magazine from other confessions. No two are exactly alike, regardless of any similarity in titles.

It is wise not to ask for a rejection before you even finish your story. Read at least one issue of the magazine for which you plan to write.

This market is eager for stories. Fewer than half of

the magazines use articles, and even fewer buy poetry (and these are chronically overstocked). Almost all the editors report they are low on fiction and eagerly look for more that they can buy.

As Ruth Beck told me, "May I say that there is an excellent opportunity to sell in the confession field. We, certainly, always have room for a well-plotted, action-filled, emotion-packed story with an original idea at its core. I wish to assure you that every manuscript submitted to us is given its due consideration. We are not only ready, but anxious, to buy material that meets our requirement."

"We desperately need new writers," says Hellen Fain. "Just a few sell over and over again. We give everyone a reading and are willing to work with writers if they show a spark."

Where else can you find a more avid market and sympathetic editors! New writers are favored, for as Miss Sandel says, "Almost none of the 300 stories we buy are ordered, even from known authors."

8

The Men's Magazine Market

Magazines published primarily for men represent a wide area of interest, so it should be comparatively easy to sell manuscripts to them. And why not? Among them are markets for fiction, articles, fillers, and even poetry. In a single year one magazine bought as many as 12,500 unsolicited manuscripts submitted by free-lance writers.

Just what are the "magazines for men"? Are they simply the cheesecake-laden, sex-ridden "girly" publications that husbands may bring home surreptitiously? Not at all, though there are some fly-by-night books of this nature. Sooner or later they pall on the readers, or the police clamp down on them. The men's magazines that endure are those that cater to many interests: adventure, exposures of wrongdoing, scandalous behavior of the prominent, sports—and, of course, men-and-women relations. An even wider area is encompassed by the outdoor and sports magazines. Perhaps these are not strictly "men's magazines," but even those that profess male exclusiveness by their titles, such as *Man to*

Man, Male, and *Stag,* carry no warning, as does the reading room of the Press Club in London, "No women are permitted to enter."

The outdoor magazines rarely intrude on the special province of the men's magazines, and indeed one of them boasts of this fact. An advertisement for *Sports Magazine* that appeared in *Advertising Age* reads: "It may come as a shock to you, but a lot of guys would rather look at Joe Namath's knees. . . . It's not so shocking when you stop and think about it. A young guy has girls around him all the time. But knees like Joe Namath's, that's a different story."

In the narrow market for fiction, it is comforting to find that several of the men's magazines are consistent buyers of fiction. This field also has its quota of magazines that publish "true" stories only. However, sometimes these are merely "based on truth." An editor told me of a big game hunter who had had a most harrowing experience with a tiger in Africa, but he was unable to fill in many gaps of names, background, and other essential details that make a story of this kind come alive for the reader. The editor bought the idea and assigned an experienced writer to do the story. It was his job to take the germ of a story, do extensive research, and build a suspenseful tale around it. The closest the writer had come to a tiger was watching one on television.

The armchair adventurer therefore has a chance to compete with the brave ones whose feats of derring-do may be distilled into 5,000 words or less. He sails the seven seas without ever leaving the security of his home or his trusty typewriter.

Whatever you write, fact or fiction, you have a receptive market, for more than 50 percent of the editors say that "over the transom" manuscripts are vital to them. Only four editors report that they rarely buy from this source. Encouraging, too, is the fact that the market is not overwhelmed by a large number of manuscripts, for 49 percent of the magazines received fewer than 1,000 to 5,000 manuscripts a year from free-lance writers. The best-known ones, like *Playboy, Esquire,* and *True,* have a much wider "choice" in that they are sent from 10,000 to 50,000 manuscripts a year. The reason *choice* is quoted is that editors by and large complain about the inferior quality and inappropriateness of all too many of the unsolicited manuscripts. There is little to choose from, leaving the editor no choice but to reject the bulk of such submissions.

Almost forlornly, R. M. Macauley, fiction editor of *Playboy,* says that his "best advice is to read the magazine. We always say that—yet it's surprising how many writers submit completely inappropriate work."

The offenders are many, as Richard Ashby, associate editor of *Knight* and *Adam Reader,* reveals: "Our biggest cause of rejection is unfamiliarity with our needs . . . and this includes agents as well as writers."

Almost without exception editors urge writers to learn something about a magazine before sending material to it. "Query first," is the admonishment of David Ivins, associate editor of *Saga.* "Have documentation of your stories. Keep your writing straightforward. Look over a few issues of *Saga* to get an idea of our needs."

When you make a sale to a man's magazine, you gain something more than a check. You gain a position of confidence that demonstrates that you can write for this market. The editor then may be inclined to turn

assignments your way. More than 50 percent of the
editors rate buying on assignment as the preferred
source of obtaining material.

The main purpose of the men's magazines is to entertain, though there is an increasing interest shown in
controversial subjects, the offbeat, and the satirical.
Only 34 percent of the magazines list sex as a primary
interest. The men's magazine group is not static. Subjects that are emphasized now may decline in interest
later, though the general character of any given magazine is not likely to alter considerably. The "need to
read" a magazine is imperative at all times.

Presumably men are more interested in sports and in
ourdoor activities than are women, but more and more
the ladies are showing a lively interest along with men.

Outdoor magazines fall into two classifications, those
of general sports and outdoors interest and those that
represent just a single sport.

The stay-at-home writer has little chance of selling to
either one, for the magazines are mainly directed to
devotés who really know the score. Therefore, these
publications are geared to give authoritative information, helpful suggestions, and pertinent data, with only
a nod to entertainment.

As Edward F. Murphy, senior editor of *Sports Afield*,
says, "Before trying to write for us, a writer should
study articles in the magazine thoroughly. He must
consider himself an expert in some branch of the outdoor field in order to write a convincing article. Good,
dramatic photographs are almost as important as the
copy."

A rejection slip is waiting for any article that "doesn't
contain plenty of helpful information that is either new

or has a new slant," says Clare Conley, editor of *Field and Stream*.

"Don't aspire to write for us," is the enigmatic statement of Ray Cave, senior editor of *Sports Illustrated*. However, this isn't the dismissal it would seem to be. Mr Cave adds these reassuring words: "Write the story the way you want to write it, the best possible way, and we'll see if it turns out to be for us. We have no set style, attitudes, approach, etc. as far as free-lance work is concerned. The one thing we look for is distinguished prose."

Important as experience in an activity may be, this alone is not always enough. Catherine E. McMullen, editor of *Better Camping*, laments the fact that campers "with years of experience do not usually provide the type of copy we want."

The practical rather than the lyrical is demanded by George S. Wells, editor of *Camping Guide* and *Trailering Guide Magazine*, who says that he wants "a down-to-earth approach, oriented to travel, and a firm acquaintance with the subject. Our writers just about have to be campers in order to approach the subject with authority. We don't care about pearls of writing but about useful information and ideas for our readers."

The majority of magazines in the sports and outdoor field are highly specialized, dealing solely with a single activity. The absolute necessity to know the subject about which one writes should be apparent to any writer. The value placed on knowledge is underscored by Frank Woolner, editor of *Salt Water Sportsman*, who says that "we prefer to rewrite an exceptional article by a well-informed fisherman, rather than to buy a polished piece by a professional journalist who doesn't know his angling. . . . Our readers are modern, scientific anglers; they want facts and up-to-date information presented in a readable manner."

Just knowing something about golf, or skiing, or any other sport may not be enough; you have to know more than the average participant in that sport. "Don't try to fake knowledge," warns Dave Wolfe, editor of *Handloader*. "If you don't know the subject, go to another market."

"All articles must reflect an *expertise* of the sport, nothing superficial," warns Patrick McNulty, managing editor of *Surfer*. "The author must know what he is talking about."

Over and over editors in this area remind writers that armchair knowledge or even simple participation is not enough. "Only authoritative articles of interest to experienced yachtsmen have a chance," says William W. Robinson, editor of *Yachting*. "We get too many features with a nautical background that have nothing to do with yachting."

The complaint of Ken Fermogle, editor of *Wheels Afield*, is similar: "We receive far too many manuscripts of overly subjective, diary-style accounts of trips people have taken in a camper or trailer that are of interest only to the people involved and fail to include information of value to others."

Editorial advice is neatly summed up by Frank T. Moss, executive editor of *Sport Fishing*, who says, "Learn to fish first."

However, even authoritative knowledge is not enough; you must also have something fresh to say. Ross Goodner, editor of *Golf*, reminds writers that "because our field is so specialized, it's difficult for writers to come up with anything new. As a result, most of the material we receive is repetitious and often downright trite. What we need is either so well written that repetition is no handicap or something with a fresh approach."

This very difficulty creates a condition of natural selection. "The ability to be creative on a subject covered hundreds of times," sagely remarks Ted Wilcox, managing editor of *Fishing & Hunting News*, "is the mark of the pro compared to the novice."

However, Jay Rakusan, editor of *Guns Magazine*, prefers that you "do not write variations of old themes."

How to please editors of the specialized sports magazines is outlined by several editors, as follows:

A. R. Harding, editor of *Fur-Fish-Game:* "Be honest and 'down to earth.'" John Gaffney, publisher of *Dive:* "Sell the sizzle, not the steak. Glamour, adventure, treasure, girls." V. Foster, publisher of *Skiing Illustrated:* "We seldom see sharp copy, fresh copy—and never *good* humor." Enzo Serafini, editor of *Skier Magazine:* "If your motivation is autobiographical, your name [had] better be Stein Eriksen or Jean-Claude Killy or you're wasting your time." Dick Aultman, editor of *Golf Digest:* "Free-lancers who don't first query an editor about the publication's needs for a specific article are wasting both their time and the editor's. Those who query and who give a thorough concept of the article rate high on my list of writers." John Gartner, executive director of *Western Outdoors* and *Southern Outdoors:* "Basic requirement for all material is *tightly written, accurate information, entertainingly presented.* Forget the dramatics and use a light touch where possible. Do not send overly long stories and expect us to cut them."

Writers who heed the foregoing suggestions are candidates for checks instead of rejection slips. Many editors are waiting, pen in hand, to sign checks for material sent them by free-lance writers. More than 50 percent of the editors in this classification buy from 33 percent to 100 percent of the manuscripts they need from free-lance writers. At least 70 percent of the editors look with some degree of interest to the coming of the mailman with the day's offerings of unsolicited manuscripts—despite the fact that most editors find that far too many submissions are poorly researched, lacking in authority, and without necessary data and interviews. They sadly comment most of all on the dull writing and lack of anything new in the bulk of what is sent them.

The need for good pictures to illustrate articles is ignored by far too many writers. As Lew Eskin, editor of *Wrestling Review,* says, "We need good pictures as well as interesting stories. Most often if a story is well written, the pictures submitted with it are of a poor quality, or the reverse is true, good pictures and poor writing. Of course, it isn't often that you find a good writer and photographer in one person, but they should get together."

The importance of illustrations is emphasized by David D. Vigren, managing editor of *Fishing World,* who says that "more free-lance submissions are returned because of inadequate illustrations of main story points than for any other reason. Plan articles from the standpoint of information *and* illustrations. They should work as one to the reader's service. Quality illustration is essential to every manuscript we buy."

All the sports and outdoor magazines use articles, though not to the exclusion of other types of material, for 40 percent use some fiction; 80 percent, fillers; and 30 percent occasionally buy verse.

This is a receptive and active market for the work of free-lance writers who know whereof they write and are professional in their craftsmanship.

9

The Book Market

        The big money may lie in getting a book published. Here's a star to hitch your wagon to! "The author of a big smash will probably make somewhere between $40,000 and $100,000 on the hardcover item that begins the great chain of success," *Life Magazine* reports. "Selection by a book club may carry an initial advance as high as $40,000, but the figure can go higher if members really take to the offering. Excerpting or condensation by a magazine can add anything from $10,000 on up, while $100,000 for paperback rights is not unusual. Nor by any means is this the end. Foreign rights constitute a shining, inestimable rivulet of gold. . . . But the biggest source of loot, however, is the movies."

It does not seem to be too difficult to write an acceptable book of some kind if you've got the patience to sit at the typewriter to pound out upwards of 40,000 words. The field is broad enough.

Publishers' Weekly reports that in 1967 there were published 1,981 novels; 2,390 juveniles; 739 books of poetry and drama; 1,502 books on religion; 6,198 general works covering art, music, philosophy, etc., and 9,067 technical books on such subjects as science, law, medicine, business, etc.—a total of 21,877 new books from 681 publishers.

One hundred trade publishers, each issuing many books a year, report in answer to our query that they had received in twelve months a total of 112,128 submissions of unsolicited manuscripts of all types, and that from this number they had purchased 1,432 manuscripts—about 1 percent of the total.

Apparently this percentage has remained fairly constant for quite some time, for George H. Doran, one of the most respected publishers of a generation ago, is quoted in *Publishing in America* as saying, "In most publishing offices, it is safe to say that not more than 1 percent of manuscripts [is] accepted, not because they are not worthy but because a publisher's output is naturally limited and many manuscripts offered do not come within the scope of the particular publisher's policy."

This gentle explanation is contradicted by John F. Marion, managing editor of Chilton Books, who says that "too many manuscripts come in that can *never* be published, and this must be because the writer has little or no self-criticism. I feel that most beginning writers are not reading enough of what is being published and with a critical eye. If they did, the manuscripts would show it." To which Edwin Seaver, editor-in-chief of George Braziller, Inc., adds this "amen": "It's not enough to be a writer—you've got to have talent, too."

Editors are willing to go out of their way to work with

writers who have ability and show a willingness to learn. You can avoid being "a face in the shadow," as the respected publisher Frederick A. Stokes once called unpublished, unknown authors. J. A. Hethrington, editor of Musson Book Company, tells you to "discuss your work with editors and publishers in person, if and when possible. Don't spend years writing in the back room if the theme, writing style or content isn't salable." There's comfort in what Charles B. Everitt, administrative editor of Little, Brown, says: "A new writer is treated like an old writer and will have exactly the same success if he is any good. We are interested in quality from any quarter."

Although editors will work with a promising writer, "Don't expect publishers to furnish detailed criticism of your writing," warns Robert J. Hill, Jr., editor of general books of Abingdon Press. "There is not time to do this with 1,200 manuscripts a year.

"Before writing a book manuscript, the author should take advantage of the training and advice available through writing classes and professional agencies. Don't ask friends to evaluate your writing. Try to accumulate a background of experience in newspaper or magazine writing before launching into a book manuscript."

The usual minimum wordage wanted by publishers is 60,000; this may seem formidable, but a constructive attitude and good working conditions can mitigate the awesomeness of the task.

Calvin Bulthuis, editor of Wm. B. Eerdmans Publishing Co., says, "Write and write some more, but before you turn your manuscript in to a publisher, make certain that you know what you are trying to do, trying to say, whom you are trying to reach. Be gainfully employed in some other kind of work. Don't depend upon royalties, etc., to pay the grocery bills. In the first place, only a very few writers earn a living by writing (and then only after some years); and in the second place, getting out of bed and punching a clock will force you to decide whether you are serious about writing."

Henry W. Simon, executive editor of Simon & Schuster, makes this practical observation: "Generally speaking, an author who has seldom or never found publication for short pieces in periodicals (fiction or nonfiction) is taking a very long gamble [in] embarking on a full-length book. He should be sure he has mastered his craft professionally (or salably) enough to warrant spending the months or years it may take to prepare a full-length book. Without a history of *some* sort of acceptance, he will find it just as hard to get a good agent as to get a publisher, and unless he knows the publishing world personally, he needs an agent to decide for him which editor and which publisher is likely to be interested in his kind of book."

Your motive in wanting to write a book is important. "Be an artist," says Jack L. Cross, executive editor of the trade book department of Steck-Vaughn. "Say what you have to say because you *have* to say it. Quit worrying about the sale of your book and don't write to 'make' it sell." Which is virtually what Dan Wickenden, editor of the trade department of Harcourt, Brace & World, says, "Work hard, type neatly, consult the dictionary, pay heed to grammar, and don't write in the hope of making money or becoming famous, but because you are *compelled* to write."

Esther K. Meeks, children's book editor of Follett

Publishing Co., thinks that "if you have good taste and judgment, based upon wide reading, *and* you have confidence in your work, you shouldn't be discouraged by rejections. Keep on submitting and keep on writing."

Perhaps as good advice as any is that offered by Robert M. Ockene, editor of Bobbs-Merrill, who says: "Take anything an editor says half-seriously."

It is encouraging that publishers *do* buy "over the transom" manuscripts, especially as 20 percent of the editors queried said that the quality of manuscripts coming to them has deteriorated, as compared to the 10 percent who discover improvement; the remaining 70 percent were unable to find any discernible change in the quality of unsolicited material.

Despite an understandable pessimism about the value of these manuscripts, apparently the publisher's answer to this problem is not the literary agent.

Only 17 percent of the editors queried declared in favor of the literary agent. They encountered an opposing vote by the 20 percent who are against cutting off the direct flow of unsolicited submissions. The remaining 63 percent want the best of two worlds. An anonymous editor quoted in *The Writer* wrote: "We're delighted when a publishable manuscript comes to us without introduction or warning. A lot of unpublished writers believe they have to be represented by a literary agent to crack a publisher's list. This simply is not true—I don't believe there has ever been a year when our list contained more agented than non-agented books."

"It is always difficult to publish an unsolicited manuscript," admits John Hess, executive editor of Meredith Press, "but we still look at unsolicited material with a reasonable amount of care."

At Harper & Row, according to Genevieve Young, assistant managing editor of trade books, "Manuscripts 'over the transom' are as welcome as those coming from agents."

Editors who are disturbed by the torrent of worthless manuscripts have diminishing patience with them. John A. Pope, Jr., managing editor of St. Martin's Press, says that "If a choice were to be made, this publisher would prefer to have all manuscripts come through bona fide agents. Out of 25 to 50 manuscripts, unsolicited, received during a *month*, only one was bought during the past *twelve months.*"

Even more gloomy is the report of D. R. Bensen, editor of Pyramid Books, who admits that "in my eight years at Pyramid we have published *two* unsolicited manuscripts, both at a time when more than half our list consisted of original books. Now we use mostly reprints, and we are *not* a market for non-agented manuscripts."

Fortunately for writers, the foregoing view is shared by very few editors.

A cool wind refreshing to both author and publisher has swept through the industry. No longer is it necessary for a writer to complete a book manuscript before he can have a fair idea whether or not it may be salable. Today most publishers, equally eager to be charged only with the responsibility to consider a portion of a manuscript, prefer to receive a query letter, followed by the submission of two or three chapters. In fact, Roland H. A. Seboldt, book editor of Concordia

Publishing House, recommends that one should "write the publisher first—before beginning a writing project."

Leo Guild, managing editor of Holloway House, asks for a little more: "I think a cleverly written synopsis as a first page would help." Allan Barnard, executive editor of Bantam Books, advocates that you should "query editors, submitting a summary and sample chapters." Raymond T. Bond, editor of Dodd Mead & Co., emphasizes a rather different value of a query when he suggests, "Have the courtesy of asking permission before sending the manuscript. Include a half-page account of the book."

Of course, the editorial purpose of the query is to cut down on reading time done by the editorial staff. Herbert Michelman, editor-in-chief of Crown Publishers, advocates another aid to the busy editor. "Obtain the opinion of a qualified person before writing to the publisher. Always send a query, including a detailed description of your manuscript before submission."

Editors may sound demanding, what with their "rules" and their peremptory rejection of precious manuscripts, but perhaps writers will be enlightened by what Willian Jovanovich wrote in his book, *Now Barabbas:* "A typical trade publisher in New York receives as many as one hundred manuscripts a week, yet he will publish but one hundred books a year; thus the rate of rejection can be as high as fifty to one. A consequence is that editors spend a better part of their days reading and discussing books they will never publish, which makes them skeptical and jaded. (The layman wonders whether all manuscripts are read straight through—and novices will sometimes submit manuscripts with transposed pages in order to find the truth of it.) Most manuscripts *are* read in their entirety, though a sensible editor recognizes that one need not eat the whole apple to know it is wormy."

Ah, when a good apple is found! "I know of no greater thrill than the discovery and the bringing to popular success of some new writer," Mr. Doran once remarked.

The willingness of editors to help writers is reflected in the sage advice they offer to aspiring writers. Observance of the following dicta of various editors will help you to avoid rejection slips:

Bernard Garfinkel, editor of Platt & Munk: "Try to learn why a book sells, what the elements of popular appeal are for a nonfiction book. As for fiction, write honestly."

Miss Jean Karl, editor of children's books for Atheneum: "Don't follow popular trends or write to a market. Be yourself and say what you want to say. Avoid the coy, the cute, the clever, the sentimental, etc., and write something of value in an honest, straightforward manner."

Judith Gilson, editorial assistant of G. P. Putnam's Sons: "We publish books that will sell, and therefore they must be of current interest to the general public. A good look at the market would give an author an idea of what to submit. We rarely go out on a limb unless a book simply hits us over the head—for example, 'Candy.'"

August Derleth, editor of Arkham House, Publishers: "Most writers simply do not practice their craft steadily enough and with enough determination to get even close to the top."

Janet A. Loranger, editor-in-chief of children's books, Charles Scribner's Sons: "It would be useful to would-be writers of juvenile books to acquaint themselves thoroughly with books already on the market. Thus they could avoid sending a publisher yet another manuscript about a Christmas tree, for example."

Ellis Amburn, senior editor of Coward-McCann, Inc.: "The conventional narrative (from Tolstoy to Wouk) is here to stay, despite recent isolated successes in the open narrative and anti-novel. Young authors should immerse themselves in the world of practical affairs— the Army, business, law, medicine, society (just like Henry James said—live, live, live!), politics, government, etc., for the larger and more anonymous our society gets, the more people—readers—want to know how it operates, from the inside. It is difficult to identify with monolithic structures today—outside of novels."

Clarkson N. Potter, editor of Clarkson N. Potter, Inc.: "Writing is a craft. Be serious about it and remember that Bernard Shaw didn't think he had mastered the language until he was over forty."

Charles N. Heckelmann, managing editor of David McKay Company: "Concentrate on the fact that a writer's first duty is to tell a good story. There is no substitute for sound, dramatic story telling. It is important to write well, with dedication and feeling and with a thorough understanding of your characters, of their motives, their hopes and needs and drives. A good writing style is important—but not at the expense of telling a sound, entertaining story."

Margaret K. McElderry, editor of children's books of Harcourt, Brace & World: "Don't try to tailor your writing to any specific 'market.' First, have something you really *want* to write about, whether it's fiction or nonfiction. Then write to the best of your ability, to please yourself."

Paul Neimark, editor-in-chief of New Classics House: "Think for yourself; write what you think honestly."

Armed with such helpful information from the editors themselves, you are instructed at least on how to fend off rejection slips. Additional tips on how to get in the editor's good graces are these: Be professional! Don't ask for a criticism, don't nag the editor, don't send in sloppy, difficult-to-read manuscripts. It would seem that such warning is unnecessary, especially as far as writers of book manuscripts are concerned, for surely anyone who undertakes to write thousands of words to be marketed would know enough to avoid the foregoing "don'ts." Were this so it would not have been necessary for Ellrose D. Zook, executive editor of Herald Press, to pass this on to writers: "Manuscripts look too carelessly prepared. Too many manuscripts repeat the same thing over and over, especially in children's fiction. Too many writers show a lack of creativity, research and careful writing and author editing."

"My best advice is to *take* advice and apply it," says Louise Crago, associate editor of United Graphics, publishers of Playtime Books, Neva Paperbacks, etc. "Every month the writers' magazines publish sound information about the craft of writing, marketing information, how to submit manuscripts, and so on; yet it seems that the majority of people who send material to us have never looked into these magazines. Either that or, what is more likely, they simply ignore it. . . . It seems that many writers are blindly stubborn and simply send out manuscripts with their fingers crossed, hoping that by some lucky break someone will publish them. This is, of course, a terrible waste of money and time for both parties, and could easily be corrected by a bit of serious study on the part of the writer."

In this chapter, editors have told you some of the requirements of successful writing and have urged you to be as professional as you can be. Having written your book, there remains one more important step to achievement—intelligent marketing. As Mrs. Frances Schwartz, editor of children's books of Abelard-Schuman, says, "Make sure that your manuscript is being submitted to a publisher who publishes that type of book."

Carol Houck, editor of W. W. Norton & Co., suggests that you "explore existing publications of the house before submitting manuscripts. This will save a lot of time and postage. See if a particular house publishes the type of fiction (especially) you have to submit."

Virtually every publisher is vexed by the submission of unsuitable manuscripts. Donald A. Wollheim, editor of Ace Books, pursues the subject when he says, "The trouble with most unsolicited writers is that they do not know their markets and that they submit unlikely works to the wrong publishers. We have certain needs —even good novels that are outside these needs will have no chance here, yet many will constantly submit such things. Most of what we buy and publish is written by authors who know what we have published in the past, know what we are looking for, and write with that in mind."

That some publishing houses issue highly specialized books should be apparent to any conscientious writer. Bern Porter, chairman of the board of Bern Porter

Books, expresses his surprise in this way: "We are internationally known and registered as American avantgarde, experimental. Yet writers send us any conceivable manuscript! Know your market before sending."

The importance of understanding a market so as to avoid unnecessary bother to editors and wastefulness on your part is made clear by what a specialized publisher tells you about his requirements. "We publish a very limited list of carefully selected and developed nonfiction and fiction," writes Don Preston, executive editor of Bernard Geis and Associates, "with heavy emphasis on promotion, publicity and advertising. Since the list is limited and the demands rather special, we can't be considered a potential market for general submissions. Queries are essential and, though all ideas are given careful consideration, writers should look over our list before trying us.

"As for the quality of unsolicited material, I can only say that we have rarely found anything in it for us, though we have seen things we've rejected on other publishers' lists, and once in a while the other publishers have been proved right. Again, our interests are pretty special, though the list has ranged widely from presidents (Harry S. Truman) to kings (Hussein of Jordan), with an admixture of such writers as Nelson Algren, Irwin Shaw, and Brendan Behan. We've done well with Art Linkletter's books, with *Sex and the Single Girl*, and with *Harlow*, and we expect to stir up some excitement in coming months."

Study of the book market is productive on two levels; it will enable you to market intelligently, and it is an investment in a market that is certain to continue. As Kenneth D. McCormick, vice-president and editor-in-

chief of Doubleday & Co., said in a recent speech to
book publishers, "The book is here to stay. . . . Content is up and growing, and this is what really counts. I
don't see anything to suggest a downward curve."

Mr. Jovanovich's summation in *Now, Barabbas* effectively serves as a conclusion to this subject:

"Although books are not the most immediate power-
ful form of expression in our society, they comprise the
freest form. Neither the press nor radio and television is
so *sure* in the enlargement and defense of intellectual
liberty. It may be argued *extenuare* that books, unlike
newspapers, are made safe from popular pressures by
being addressed to the few; and that the buyer of books
exercises an individual choice—tempered by high price
—whereas the newspaper subscriber receives issue
after issue on trust and without prior examination or
renewal. . . . Intellectual freedom is not, in the long
view, measured by writers, but by readers."

10

The Specialized Magazine Market

Do you know there is a magazine published just for postcard collectors? And if there isn't one published for collectors of bottle-caps or old-fashioned hat pins, just make it known that there is a fairly large potential readership, and someone will start such a magazine. In the special interest field there exist magazines dealing with almost anything that people find of interest.

A quick glance reveals such specialized interests as history, health, world affairs, nature, pets, home service, art and music, hobbies, and amusements represented by one or more magazines. *Printing Impressions* reports that "special interest magazines, consumer publications that help readers get the most from their hobbies, are the most successful in the publishing field. These magazines are cashing in on a fifty-billion-dollar wave resulting from spending on leisure-time pursuits."

Naturally, where there are so many publications the demand for manuscripts to fill the thousands of pages is great, especially as most of the publications receive from free-lance writers as few as 100 to 1,000 manuscripts a *year*. This isn't a large supply from which to draw. Only nine periodicals among those responding to our questionnaire reported they receive in a year from 2,500 to 5,000 unsolicited manuscripts. Just three were sent 5,000, and out of some 60 magazines only one was flooded with 10,000 unsolicited manuscripts.

Although no mother lode, the specialized magazines are worth digging into, for most of them are very receptive to writers and yield a comparative abundance of acceptances over rejections. A cross section of these journals shows that 34 percent buy in excess of half of all their material from "over the transom," and 30 percent of all the editors look upon this source as important to them in filling the ever-demanding pages. The total buying is in excess of 6.5 percent from the 75,500 submissions of manuscripts. This is a better average than that of most market groups.

Though the percentage may seem low, editors bought in a single year 5,047 unsolicited manuscripts, an average of 87 by each publication. Of course, some bought many more, and others bought very few indeed.

Buying would be much higher were free-lance writers more conscientious in their craftsmanship and in their selection of potential markets. Carlette M. Winslow, managing editor of *Suburban Life,* complains that "most of the manuscripts submitted are on a very amateurish level. Some of the poetry and fillers are unbelievably bad."

You can't fool or entice editors with shoddy material. "Don't do a once-over-lightly and think the editor won't know it," warns N. N. Fuller, editor of *Fate.* "Detailed, documented studies are needed with *who, what, where,* and *when* supplied."

When writing for the specialized magazines, there is one towering point that should orient any writer: Readers of these publications are knowledgeable and want to learn more about their special interest through reading. Opinions (unless you are a recognized authority) are out; specific information is in. But you cannot rely on easily accessible information, for the chances are that such material is common knowledge. William C. Davidson, associate editor of *Flower & Garden Magazine,* says, "Dig into your subject and be specific about it. Follow good writing habits. Write in a direct and in a 'how-to-do-it' manner—about something people can use. Do not try to 'kid' anyone by writing pages of 'double talk.' "

Most of the specialized magazines are very serious about their subject and are not inclined toward the frivolous or the merely entertaining. All, naturally, use articles, but only 28 percent use fiction, and 30 percent occasionally use verse. Fillers, if they deal with the specific area of the magazine's interest, are used by 38 percent. You don't have to be deadly serious (meaning, *dull*), for as Haven H. LaSohn, director of Public Relations Membership Services of *Mobile Living,* says, "A little humor is good, but don't try to be too funny. When a 'statement of fact' is made, be sure it is realistic and capable of documentation."

Other editors have similar feelings, as indicated by Austin G. Paulnack, editor of *Syracuse University Alumni News,* who says, "Know your topic; research thoroughly, have a good style and command of English. Don't be afraid of humor—and think."

The specialized market would be more active buyers of material from free-lance writers if writers were less hasty in feeding manuscripts into the mails. Nobody would think of doing a slam-bang copy of a shirt, one sleeve longer than the other, material spotted, and offer this product to a dry goods store or a man's shop. But this is exactly the kind of product that far too many writers thoughtlessly send to editors, unrealistically thinking that somehow it might sell. This type of writer may as well bypass the specialized magazines.

"Read several recent issues of the magazine," advises Erwin M. Rosen, executive editor of *Motor Trend Magazine,* "and try to determine the preferred direction or emphasis desired. Respect the specialized technical knowledge required, the lack of which is difficult to make up for even with intensive research."

This market intimidates only the lazy or the moribund, for, as Bob Gray, editor and publisher of *Horseman, the Magazine of Western Riding,* says, "A good writer or reporter can learn this field quickly if he applies himself. But it takes the basic skills—knowledge of how to interview, how to organize material, how to keep the language simple. The technique is right in the magazine for any free-lancer sharp enough to read and learn."

It is no wonder that some editors despair. Our poll revealed that thirty-five editors found unsolicited material to be too superficial to deserve serious attention; thirty rejected manuscripts because they were based on insufficient research; and the same number found them either dully written or without anything new to say. As many as twenty-four editors were disturbed by the lack of authority to back up personal opinions. The need for statistics, pertinent examples, and interviews with key persons were other reasons for promptly rejecting manuscripts.

These shortcomings are spelled out by editors. David Aldrich, editor-in-chief of *Bravo* and *Bravo/Carnegie Hall*, says that "most free-lance material lacks focus. Interesting angles are missing, usually resulting in bad titles. Material should be of interest to a national readership."

"Articles must be imaginative," insists Don E. Bower, executive editor of *Colorado Magazine*. "Use lots of quotes (dialogue) and make our nonfiction believable —but also exciting."

R. B. Kirkpatrick, editor of *National Wildlife*, gets down to fundamentals when he says, "learn something. Send a sensible query. Produce a good article in professional style. Help find photographs to illustrate it." A plea that never should apply to a writer who aspires to professionalism is made by Lyda L. Mosier, editor of *Success:* "Please reread your manuscript for grammatical, spelling and typing errors. Complete a trend of thought. Plan good conclusions."

Respect a magazine's readers by talking to them on their own plane. A condescending attitude will earn you nothing more than a rejection slip—with the editor's disgust. This is expressed in strong words by R. H. MacDonald, executive editor of *The Western Producer*, who tells you that "our readers are farmers but not hicks. Neither are they New York neurotics. They believe in hard work, God, and being good neighbors. They like a beginning, middle and end in their stories."

The editorial demand, ubiquitous in its repetition, is "know the market to which you send material." So here we go again!

"Writers should study copies of magazines and become familiar with the type of material used, length, etc., before submitting manuscripts," says Henry F. Henrich, the editor of *Sunshine Magazine.* "The bulk of manuscripts we receive are not suited to our editorial needs." John L. Smith, editor of *V.F.W. Magazine,* says that "free-lance writers should study and know the publication to which they are submitting a manuscript. At least 75 percent of the material we receive is not geared to our publication. There is also a trend today toward opinion as opposed to fact in material sent us. We are not interested in unsolicited opinion. Dirty manuscripts that have obviously made the rounds are a pet peeve."

"Get a copy of our magazine and learn our primary interests," advises Gary Adamson, managing editor of *The Optimist Magazine.* "Please—no articles of personal opinion strung out into an article. . . . Stop avoiding the issues and problems of the day. I automatically reject any article that is padded."

Naturally, the lower paying magazines, for the most part, rely more strongly on the unsolicited free-lance manuscript. The rate of payment is remarkably broad, ranging from a meager 1¢ a word to 20¢ a word; from a flat payment of $5 to a nice round figure of $700.

Although a slight majority of these magazines pay writers when their material is accepted, almost 50 percent of them pay on publication. Low pay, all too often, carries with it payment delayed until the manuscript is printed. This unhappy combination is the load the new writer sometimes must bear, for the established professional is unlikely to submit material either to very low paying magazines or to those that pay after publication.

The aspiring writer should heed the advice of editors to be thorough in research, to hunt diligently for something new or a fresh slant, to write with enthusiasm, to authenticate personal opinions, and to be intelligent in the selection of markets.

11

The Consumer Magazine Market

Writing for the consumer magazines brings up visions of seeing your name in print in the big slicks or women's magazines, and checks of astronomical amounts. The term "consumer magazines" means those magazines that appeal to a general readership. Magazines that have a circulation of several million subscribers are certainly general. Many of them are printed on smooth paper (such as enamel, English finish, etc.); hence the term "slicks." Circulation ranges from a few thousand to as many as ten million. When you have appeared a few times in the big consumer magazines you are in a fair way to becoming nationally known.

That's what those writers who already have earned "big names" know. And they are not unaware that a story or article in these publications can command a price of $5,000 or more. Naturally you want some of this clover, too. Can you avoid rejection slips?

A writer I know sold quite a few stories for two or three cents a word and then decided that he was ready for the big time. But in back of his mind was the thought that if the story missed at *Saturday Evening Post* or *Redbook*, he could always sell it to one of his regular markets. He never made the grade, because merely polishing his stories a little more wasn't enough. Mentally, he could never get out of the conventional run of stories he wrote, and all the rewriting and shining up he did could not make the essential difference. Another writer friend always wrote stories that were a little better than the ones before. He was orienting his thinking toward distinctive stories, and when he had gained more experience in writing he began selling to the large consumer magazines. This is one way to avoid rejection slips in this area: read and analyze the markets you want to write for, and work steadily toward them. If the need or desire to sell to lesser markets is demanding, don't try just to get by, but offer the editor the best you can do.

The consumer group is comprised of somewhat fewer than 100 magazines, covering such subjects as the family, women's interests, brides, fashion, service wives, government workers, international and internal affairs, satire, exposés, and a knowledgeable or smart approach to all subjects. Rates paid—in almost all cases, on acceptance—range from 2¢ to 7¢ a word; from $25 for a piece of work to $5,000. While non-fiction articles dominate the kinds of material bought, some of these magazines use also long and short fiction, poetry, special features, and fillers. The really displaced type of manuscript is not poetry, as many persons think, but the essay. This once favored form of expression is today almost totally neglected by this market area.

Most of the consumer magazines insist upon the necessity for a query prior to submission of an article, but this is not a requirement for fiction. You can obtain a sympathetic reading without any preliminary permission from the editor. This may be an advantage to you, especially if you aren't very good at writing query letters.

An encouraging note is this from Naomi Lewis, fiction editor of *Good Housekeeping:* "Remember that our job is to find fiction material the magazine can use, and to that end, it matters little to us *where* we find them—whether they come from agents or out of the unsolicited manuscript pile. We are not, however, running a writers' school, and we do expect the would-be writer to do the minimum part of his job—double-spaced typing, pages numbered, name and address on each page, self-addressed stamped envelope for return included, and all the other niceties that make our reading lives easier. At least one-third of the manuscripts we receive are in sloppy and unprofessional condition. That never happens with agented material, of course, and we also know that the agent has some reason to believe we will buy the story, or else he would not be wasting *his* time—from the agent's point of view."

The message is clear. Look upon your story as an agent would; unless it is properly prepared, unless you are reasonably sure that it is in harmony with what is being published in the particular magazine, don't send it. A poorly prepared, inappropriate manuscript not only will be rejected, but it will also make the editor a little more skeptical about unsolicited free-lance manuscripts.

Despite the more rigid requirements of the large consumer magazines, and a weakness for "big names," interest in the new writer remains strong and potent.

Margaret Treadwell, a member of the editorial staff of *Redbook,* puts it this way: "We want a good plot, i.e., a plot in which characters are put into tension and motion and are enabled to bring out their most interesting possibilities. The character can be of any age, sex, etc., as long as he is one the reader can become fond of. A writer is on the right track if he writes because he *cares* about people, observes them, and has something to say about them. These requirements of plot and character are another way of saying we want good writing, even though it is hard to achieve. For authors ever heading in the right direction, we offer every editorial encouragement and assistance."

Miss Treadwell's "formula" for successful fiction is a timeless one and is relevant to most good stories.

Some writers who have garnered a collection of rejection slips maintain that editors of large magazines take delight in sending rejection slips to unknown writers, that actually these editors are committed to buy only from established authors. As the statements from editors reveal, this is far from the truth. Even the deepest adulation for success, and this from the biggest magazines, must give way to the need to nurture new talent to replace the inevitable removal from the table of contents of writers called by death.

It is true, alas, that the demand for fiction has slimmed down to a mere shadow of its former self. Today among the 100 consumer magazines only 38 percent use fiction. Obviously, the prevailing demand is for nonfiction, and this trend is likely to continue well into the future.

It may happen that any talented writer can sell a short story to the slicks, but this is less likely in the case of important nonfiction. Experience is needed in doing research and in conducting interviews, supported by skill in selecting and presenting material. Quite a few editors prefer to buy an idea from a new writer and then assign an experienced author to prepare the article. Indeed, a recent survey showed that 70 percent of all consumer-magazine editors prefer giving assignments to writers with whom they know they can work rather than buying an article from a new writer.

The editor's way of saying this is reflected in what Donald L. McKinney, chief articles editor of *Saturday Evening Post,* wrote me: "Read the magazine carefully over half a dozen issues. Submit ideas in letter form, directed to a specific editor. I would never advise a writer to go ahead and write a piece without definite encouragement from a magazine."

In order to avoid rejection slips from the large consumer magazines, query the editor before you write an article. If the editor agrees to pay you for your idea, not for your article, you may be wise to accept the offer. In any event observe the dictum of Richard Kaplan, associate editor of *Ladies' Home Journal,* who says forcefully: "Read the magazine! We get so many suggestions for stories we have just done—or stories we wouldn't do in a million years. Also, without intending to be unkind, we cannot take time to be a training school for writers; yet so many earnest free-lancers think this is what we're here for. *This* is the kind of free-lancer we'd like to discourage."

Reading the magazines you want to write for not only helps you to get the "feel" of them, but also tells you what has been used so that you can avoid duplication.

The term "consumer magazine" also embraces other than those publications with vast circulations. There are about 80 "books" appealing to a more or less homogenous audience, which is in some instances quite small. Among such publications are those dealing with home and garden, child care, and intellectual interests. The circulation figures of some of these are limited and so are the rates of payment for material. Consequently, the intensity of competition is less.

The National Writers Club survey of all consumer magazines reveals that 26 percent of them receive fewer than 1,000 manuscripts a year; 30 percent, fewer than 5,000; 26 percent, from 5,000 to 10,000; and 18 percent (mainly consisting of the large circulation publications) from 10,000 to 50,000 a year.

Although some magazines receive comparatively few manuscripts, this does not mean that the editors are willing to take just anything to fill up their books. There are other sources from which to obtain good material, even if the staff themselves have to write it!

While most of the editors profess no great preference for manuscripts sent to them by respected agents, there is no doubt that editors of the large magazines have a certain fondness for what an agent sends over. In her fresh and stimulating way, Helen Gurley Brown, editor of *Cosmopolitan,* tells why. "Whether the completed, unsolicited manuscript comes from an agent or 'over the transom,' as they say, doesn't make any difference to me. The only reason you pay attention to agents is that they have prescreened stuff in a way and you know it won't be THAT bad when it's in one of their green, blue or pink folders. . . . They can't afford to have you say how could Marian have sent me this piece of junk;

she must have lost her mind and so they send you *possible* stuff anyway. . . ."

Mrs. Brown buys from the "slush pile," she says: "Perhaps 10 percent of all the stuff that goes into the book was unsolicited completed manuscripts. It would be dandy to buy more, but we don't receive that many good ones. Of the 10 percent of unsolicited stuff we buy, about half of it is from rank amateurs who have *something* about them. . . . some kind of experience in their lives nobody else had exactly that way. . . . something kind of paint-fresh and different and you almost can't afford to pass it up. But oh the ditchdigging crumby work that goes into fixing it up. . . . You almost swear off. It isn't easy to find rewriters and it gets less and less profitable to take manuscripts from amateurs just for the idea contained because you put too many staff man-hours getting it in shape."

In order to hold its readership and influence advertisers, the consumer magazine, perhaps more than other kinds, must keep abreast of the changing times. Few magazines are static—and when they are, they are likely to go the way of the lamented *Collier's* and *American,* which, according to some authorities, lacked a sharp up-to-date "personality" and hence were unable to lure advertisers from similar but more progressive magazines.

Nevertheless, there is some solid, unchangeable ground. No matter how much they may change in editorial policy, the women's magazines will always appeal to women, those dealing with international affairs will be interested in developments important politically and economically. The reason for the constant admonition to "read several issues of the magazine" is to urge writers to keep up with the contemporary variation or slant of any given publication.

The following ideas expressed by editors reflect not only the contemporary requirements but also anticipate what probably will be the dominant policy for some time to come. In order to give you a cross section of the characteristic consumer magazines, listen to what the editors have to say.

"We want well-researched, well-written articles with a strong, fresh and newsworthy Canadian angle," reports *Maclean's Magazine.* "We'll also consider 'universal' satire and short believable pieces of domestic humor (500–1000 words). All we can suggest for would-be contributors is that they become familiar with *Maclean's Magazine,* which is available on newsstands in most major U.S. cities. Most manuscripts submitted to us from the U.S. have no Canadian angle and don't meet our requirements because the writers have not bothered to find out what we're in the market for. The ones that have a Canadian angle often don't have any topicality or any particular reason for being published. In 1965, of the hundreds and hundreds of suggestions and/or unsolicited manuscripts received from the States, we used one. This author sold us again in 1966, but only one other unsolicited manuscript or suggestion was accepted."

"Free-lancers should realize that we don't want standard my-trip pieces," maintains Stephen Wilkinson, assistant to the editor of *Holiday.* " 'What I did and saw in Scotland, plus the pictures I took. . . .' Nor do we want to send an author off on an expensive journey in hopes that it will produce an article, unless we're quite familiar with his past work—preferably both fiction and nonfiction. Finally, article queries that begin, 'Next month I am going to Outer Hebrides. . . .' don't work out, for there must be a reason for *that* writer to do a piece on *that* place—is he a sailor? a Scotsman? an islands expert? Or just another free-lancer trying to sell an idea?"

Magazine policies may change with a new editor; emphasis may be placed on different aspects or on new developments, but the basic purpose of a magazine is unlikely to be altered substantially. Therefore, what the editors say today will hold good for some time to come.

For example, a magazine edited for young women will change with changing fashions in dress and behavior, but what Ellen A. Stoianoff, fiction and poetry editor of *Mademoiselle*, says about her periodical has long-distance validity. "*Mademoiselle's* audience is primarily comprised of intelligent, college-educated young women between 18 and 25 years of age. We publish articles on current, controversial topics of interest to this age group. For fiction and poetry, literary quality is the sole criterion. We place no restrictions on theme, plot or characterizations."

The editor of *Mile High Underground* reminded me that the demonstrating, long-haired, LSD-experimenters may be the mayors and legislators of tomorrow who will bring about changes in social legislation. Youth is in the ascendancy and the more articulate ones are likely to be the new leaders. The spirit of youth is dominant. As Lawrence C. Goldsmith, special features editor of *Family Circle,* said, "Think young. Avoid the commonplace. We need stimulating, provocative, and helpful features of service to the young homemaker who is interested in broadening her intellectual horizons."

A magazine for parents joins the march to greater individuality, eschewing the trite-advice-to-moms-and-dads syndrome. *Parents' Magazine,* according to Barbara V. Hertz, managing editor, wants articles that report "new trends and significant research findings in education and in mental and physical health . . . articles encouraging informed citizen action on matters of social concern." And Phyllis B. Katz, associate editor of this magazine, adds: "If you seriously want to break into this particular field, keep trying. For the person who brings knowledge and skill to a specialized field, there is a good chance for success."

Youth rules the roost at *Redbook,* writes Robert J. Levin, articles editor: "We can always use good, strong narratives built around themes and characters of interest to our young, married readers."

There may or may not always be a Deutschland, as a huge electric sign in West Berlin proclaims, but there always will be babies—and magazines that tell mothers what and how to do for them.

"I am always looking for articles about child care," says Beth Waterfall, editor of *Mothers' Manual,* "child-rearing, education, health, experiences with children, father's role with children, new developments in psychology and children's learning that are well written and show research into recent research. I appreciate a carefully typed manuscript (no misspellings, please) that includes properly documented references to sources of information; for example, 'a University of Chicago professor recently wrote. . . .' I want to know his name, what he wrote, when he wrote it and where. Too many unsolicited manuscripts are sketchy or try to cover too many subjects. A well-developed story that moves from one thought to another with good transitions and does not repeat the same premise in different ways is appreciated."

No two magazines are exactly alike, as pointed out. *Mothers' Manual,* dealing with babies, places emphasis on the child. *Your New Baby,* according to Betty Madan, managing editor of the magazine, though also dealing with babies, places more emphasis on the parents.

"We want articles of interest to new and expectant parents," Miss Madan reports. "Baby care, infant growth and development, health, safety; family relations, new mother, new parent aspects; home management; pregnancy. We use also shorter length features, preferably with a light touch about personal experiences."

Mrs. Martha Bluming, editor of *American Baby* and *Mothers-to-Be and Infant Care,* underscores the difference between her magazines and similar ones in this way: "Our articles deal with pre- and postnatal care or on young children's development—written from a paramedical point of view—by professional writers with a strong background in this area. Stay away from sentimental first-person articles; even personal experience pieces *can* be written objectively and with constructive conclusions!"

The differences between lay and religious publications of this type are indicated by what Mrs. Wilma L. Shaffer, editor of *The Christian Mother,* says: "Keep the motto in mind: 'A guide to Christian child training.' Inspiration without being preachy; entertaining without being too corny and sentimental. We want a refreshing new approach to old problems and pleasures of mothers and family life. . . . Query letters waste my time. I'd rather see the article." *The Christian Mother* advertises that it is a "real 'bridge builder' between your church and the homes of your congregation and community."

In the consumer magazines are excitement, stimulation, information, and practical advice. It is a market area for the really serious writer whose research is thorough, whose writing reveals a pride of good workmanship. A portion of these magazines has a rejection-slip curtain between them and new writers, but it is more imaginary than real if you are truly good enough at your job of writing. Many of these magazines rely heavily on unsolicited free-lance manuscripts; all buy some material from this source. The National Writers Club survey shows that 23 percent of the editors buy 75 percent of their manuscript needs from the "slush pile"; 7 percent, half of what they buy; 17 percent buy one-fourth of their material from free-lance writers; a little more than half of the magazines buy 25 percent or less "over the transom"; only 2 percent rarely buy from this source.

When you want to write an article for the consumer magazines, it is best, with few exceptions, to work on a speculation basis, that is, by telling the editor what your idea is and offering to write the article without advance payment or obligation, pending his final acceptance. When you are an established author, the editor may assign an article subject to you, and very likely he then will make some advance payment. When you reach this highly desirable stage, you will be one of the editor's fair-haired boys, for 70 percent of all the editors of consumer magazines prefer to buy material they need on assignment.

When you send a story or article to these editors without a reasonable acquaintance with their magazines, very likely you are doing nothing more than increasing the boredom and anguish of editors who already are dubious about the value of unsolicited freelance manuscripts, as 37 percent of the editors now are, not to mention the 3 percent of them who regard these manuscripts as a nuisance.

The consumer magazines may be your royal road to success if—and only if—you travel well equipped for the arduous journey.

12

The Television Market

In the United States there are 644 commercial TV stations, and the number is more likely to increase than to decrease. In 56,049,190 homes there are one or more television sets. What an audience to write for!

It is no wonder that television is the modern Pied Piper whose cash-register tunes lure thousands of would-be writers. You get on a national hookup, after which your story is rerun, perhaps forever after, and you continue to collect royalties.

Enticing? You're right, you sure are.

But what's the catch? Yes, there is one. Selling a play to a TV studio is about the hardest job a writer has, though the difficulty is common also to other types of plays, stage and film.

The first problem is that most studios will return manuscripts unopened unless they are sent by recognized agents. The second problem is that there is very little chance of selling an occasional drama or comedy, no matter how good it is or how "recognized" your agent may be.

A story editor advises that "in any case the best thing to do is to aim for one show. Get as many scripts for that show as possible."

However, this is only one facet of salability. Sixty percent of the editors replying to our questionnaire say they want scripts submitted to them in teleplay form. This means that the writer must undertake a specialized study.

Philip Saltzman, producer of 20th Century-Fox–TV, says, "Learn to write for TV—especially in a classroom. When this is accomplished, submit plays to a recognized agent. An agent is still the entré to the world of TV writing, and he can get editors and producers to read material, then set up meetings, then get the tyro to write on assignment."

Very few story editors will consider a mere synopsis, and not many favor a full narrative development, as in a story designed for a magazine or even as a stage play.

It is clear that the aspiring television writer should learn the required technique to use in presenting his story. No longer is it possible, if it ever was, simply to dash off a story in some form and find a TV market for it. "Study the medium," urges Paul Cahill, director of community relations, Station WBBM-TV. "Too many scripts are written for film, too few for the studios. Concentrate on character development."

Logically, most of the studio editors recommend taking a good course in teleplay writing to learn the required technique. The next largest group suggest that the writer get as many published credits as he can, for these serve to demonstrate that the writer has professional writing ability. There may even be possibilities of adapting a published work for television. Sidney Marshall, story editor of *Voyage to the Bottom of the Sea* (20th Century-Fox–TV), has another idea: "Work in the industry. Learn the basic craft. Persevere, and write, write, write!"

Despite the fact that most editors and producers think that new writers should be encouraged, not a single one we queried believes that the chances to succeed in writing for television are any better than fair! Edward Barry Roberts, a former story editor for CBS and an author of TV plays, says in *The Writer*, "The important thing for the individual beginning television playwright is to be ready with the indispensable knowledge of *how* to write a television play when his opportunity comes."

The pessimistic present must not be taken for a preview of the future, for change is constant in every market. One must have the fortitude to prepare now for an uncertain future. Just what the situation is today perhaps is best told by John Hawkins, story editor of *Bonanza* (NBC), who says that "the market for the free-lance writer is narrowing steadily—more prime time is given to feature pictures, to more specials. The top writers earn a lot of money, but the number is fewer than in years past. If you're going to battle the windmill, be well prepared and well bank-rolled, and most important: be smart, tough and lucky."

In the welter of pessimism exuded by most story editors, only one holds out a rather cautious optimism. Lenore Clare, supervising editor, script department, of the Canadian Broadcasting Corporation, wrote me that "The Canadian Broadcasting Corporation does not require that a script must be submitted by an agent, nor are release forms necessary. This department reads everything that comes in and those scripts showing promise are forwarded to any one, or many, in rotation, of five production centers across Canada. Any writer showing promise will receive detailed editorial assistance from this department with a view to developing the producible script. We should also like to point out that we do not waste our time or the writer's on people who show no talent, but their scripts are carefully read first. . . . A qualified script of any type may be purchased although that particular type might not happen to be what they are looking for at the moment."

Coming back to the United States: can you live in Keokuk, Iowa, and still succeed as a writer for television? Unlikely, say most of the editors. "It depends," amends Story Editor Mark Weingart, "if one wishes to make a living at it or not. If one wishes to make a living, it is almost imperative to live near the market place. For example, Los Angeles. On the other hand, if one wishes merely to enhance his living it is possible to write in another location. In any case, the best thing to do is to aim for one show. Get as many scripts for that show as possible, and write full-length scripts in the hope that some producer will find merit in them and offer encouragement, if not an outright purchase."

In the voting of editors as to the cities where it is most advantageous for the TV script writer to live, Los Angeles won easily, followed some lengths away by New York, and with Chicago running a poor third.

The alert writer will be on the watch for TV contests and for special programs catering to new writers. For example, the Columbia Broadcasting System started the Repertoire Workshop, "an experimental approach on behalf of five CBS owned stations," according to

Joan Fiore, producer of Repertoire Workshop, Philadelphia, "those in New York, Los Angeles, Chicago, St. Louis, as well as WCAU-TV (Philadelphia), toward the discovery and development of unknown talent among writers as well as performers. . . . We shall read and consider any film scripts, teleplays, short stage plays or musical works. . . . We are interested in the sensitive, the thoughtful, the experimental approaches to our medium, rather than traditional, 'escapist' entertainment formulas."

Most of the TV studios that look at unsolicited freelance manuscripts insist upon the execution of the standard release form to accompany any submitted material.

The reason for the release is spelled out by Henry J. Schaefer of Station WBBM-TV: "Before anyone in our Program Department can examine your material, we will have to obtain your signature on a Release Form. This is necessary not only for your protection but for ours as well. As you probably realize, we receive each day a vast amount of unsolicited mail containing program ideas, suggestions, manuscripts—and in our own interest we have to be most scrupulous in safeguarding the rights of the author. . . . Because of the great number of outside ideas that are submitted to us as well as those we develop and explore on our own, it is very possible that we may have already considered suggestions that are similar to that you wish to submit and have found them unsuitable for our purposes."

Just what is a release form? Quoted are the two essential paragraphs relating to the studio's responsibilities to the author and the author's willingness to take a reasonable attitude toward material used by the studio that may be similar to his own. The excerpt follows:

> You will not make any use of my material unless you shall first negotiate with me compensation for such use. I agree, however, that your use of material containing elements similar to or identical with those contained in my material shall not obligate you to negotiate with me nor entitle me to any compensation if, because such elements are not new or novel, or were not originated by me, or because other persons (including your employees) have submitted or prepared or may hereafter submit or prepare material containing similar or identical elements, or because of any other reason you determine that you have an independent legal right to use such material.
>
> If you determine that you have the legal right to use material similar to or identical with mine, or containing elements similar to or identical with those contained in my material, without the payment of any compensation to me and proceed to use the same, and if I disagree with your determination (such disagreement to be indicated in writing to you no later than sixty [60] days after your first use of such material), I agree that if you so elect, the controversy between us shall be submitted to the New York Supreme Court for determination pursuant to the New York Simplified Procedure for Court Determination of Disputes.

Fear of plagiarism or piracy of one's material is almost always unfounded. On the other hand, TV editors have been plagued with the possibility of lawsuits because of the use of story ideas, or scenes in stories, that are similar to those sent in by free-lance writers. Such duplications are inevitable—and almost certainly innocent. The release form is the studio's protection against unwarranted lawsuits. It does not deprive the writer of anything.

Considerable consternation among viewers and writers, too, is evoked by what is seen on television. Edward W. Barrett, dean of the graduate school of journalism, Columbia University, deplores a condition in which TV executives "have become the captives of commercial forces. They find themselves under pressure to seek the approval of their directors, stockholders, and social peers." Rod Serling, one of the most capable writers for television, says he has abandoned the medium because it has too many taboos, too many restrictions and is too timorous to command his efforts.

These are worrisome thoughts about the medium for which so many writers yearn to write. Ray Abel, producer-director of Repertoire Workshop, WCBS-TV, says, "Accept the restrictions of the medium (technical as well as content) and find a way to write *well* despite what might at first seem to be a handicap. The handicap is here to stay!"

13

The Newspaper Syndicate Market

An actor dreams of seeing his name in lights on Broadway. Most aspiring writers dream of doing a syndicated column that would appear in 500 newspapers throughout the land. What could be sweeter than to write one piece, just 400 words, and get paid for it 500 times!

Editor & Publisher lists 288 syndicates that use feature material. It should be a cinch, especially as each handles one or more columns, to sell to one of them. King Features Syndicate boasts that it distributes 116 editorial features, "and we keep on adding great new features every year."

Well, you've toyed with the idea of doing a column, so why not give King a chance to add yours to their burgeoning list?

King, however, tells newspaper editors that it is No. 1 in "Big Name" features. Someone is always taking the joy out of life!

Writer's Market lists only 64 syndicates of *all kinds* that express any interest at all in free-lance material. In the book *Complete Guide to Newspaper Syndication* is this statement: "According to the president of one of the leading syndicates, of more than 1,000 features submitted each year to his organization, not more than one-tenth of one percent is acceptable. At this estimate, one's chances of ever becoming syndicated are *only* one in 100,000!"

Discouraging? No. Gloomy? Yes, but not hopeless. What has happened to the "good old days" when syndicates bought short stories, and a new writer had a reasonably good chance of breaking into at least a few newspapers? Elmer Roessner, editor-in-chief of the Bell-McClure Syndicate, explains the current situation this way: "Syndication is not an expanding field because practically no newspaper is increasing its feature space. A new feature must be so good that it knocks other features out of a hundred papers or so. And, boy, that takes great creativity."

Mergers and the high cost of paper have taken their toll. Nevertheless, our recent poll reveals that 47 percent of the syndicate editors *encourage* unsolicited freelance submissions; the other 53 percent accept this material reluctantly or discourage such submissions. Actual purchases from this source were made by 20 percent of the editors; another 40 percent bought some material, though infrequently. Most of the editors want to continue to receive submissions from free-lance writers, and only 11 percent consider the material submitted a nuisance.

There are 12,000 weekly newspapers in the United States, some with a circulation of less than 5,000. These and smaller periodicals, neighborhood and give-away papers, offer you a pretty good chance of convincing an editor to use your column. Often this will be without payment, but it gives you a chance to get into print, and there is at least a remote possibility that a syndicate editor will see your work and like it well enough to make you an offer.

I've seen a good many columns of this sort and find it necessary to issue a warning. A local editor of a small-time sheet may want to favor you, or he may have some space that needs filling; at no cost to him, what can he lose? So he may not be discriminating, or he may not know any better; the stuff that goes into some of these columns shouldn't be printed even in invisible ink. The "poems" don't rhyme and are complete strangers to rhythm; the articles deal in platitudes and poor grammar. This wouldn't make any great difference to anyone if the writers of the columns didn't think that because they are "published" they must be pretty good and therefore can go knocking at the doors of syndicates.

It's an important start to have a column printed— anywhere, and for little or no remuneration—but pride in workmanship is essential. W. Robert Walton, editor of the Hall Syndicate, supports this idea when he says that "the big majority of successful syndicate columns originate from a single 'home' newspaper. It is the readership such columns engender among that newspaper's readers that leads to syndication." As this points out, a column of yours that receives the recognition of print has been given no real recognition at all unless it gains an acceptance from readers. As James L. Freeman, managing editor of United Feature Syndicate, puts it: "First achieve publication on a regular basis by a single newspaper or magazine in order to become known and gain a following."

Of course, the ideal is to get started with a large-circulation newspaper. The editor of your home town metropolitan journal can be approached personally. If you've got a fresh idea, he may give you a chance to prove the reader-acceptance of your material. Dorothy Kostka thought that women over fifty comprise a fertile area for advice, information, and inspiration, so she discussed the idea with the editor of "Contemporary," a feature section of *The Denver Post*. It was something different and truly helpful; it has been running weekly for several years and may be a candidate for national distribution.

This is the way to go about it, if you can: "Get your material published in a large metropolitan newspaper," says William D. Bonner, editor of Bonner Features Syndicate, "and then seek syndication by sending tear sheets along with a letter from the editor."

Alas, it is difficult to heed Kurt Singer, general manager of the BP Singer Features, who tells you: "Don't try syndication unless you are well known."

Unless you are nationally known or an authority on a given subject, you are almost certain to garner rejection slips if you write about health, politics, business, child-rearing, or investments. You are highly unlikely to get a sympathetic hearing from the editor, because he knows that readers want *authoritative* advice on such matters.

Editors would be more receptive to free-lance submissions if writers would get out of the rut in which so many are. "Your material must be fresh, well-done and of general interest," says Mildred M. Bellah, executive editor of McNaught Syndicate. "Find a new field, develop your own style," says Stanleigh Arnold, editor of Chronicle Features Syndicate.

Rhoda Lewis, executive secretary of Oceanic Press Service, goes into detail to instruct anyone who aspires to do a continuing column: "We would like to make one strong point—that the curse of all submissions remains that 99 percent of the incoming material is not geared to our needs. Things we need and can buy or sell within five minutes we never get—like, a chess column, women's dress patterns, articles and pix on interior decoration, articles and pix on hair fashions, *authorized* interviews with world-famous figures, and car repair columns.

"As you see, everyone needs specialized features— and they are now staff-produced—and free-lance writers just love to send in general stories, short stories, stories about themselves, and stories of local, regional and limited interest. The formula which works for us says: Any feature must be of interest for New York, the center of the U.S. publishing industry; Finland, far out in Europe: if it is of interest to Finland it will be of interest to all Europe and the British Commonwealth; India: if it is of interest to India it will be of interest to all of Asia and Africa. A syndicate cannot afford to distribute only in the USA and Canada. We have to have the revenue from the entire free world, if possible."

Anything that interests teenagers has a particular "in" if it is different. The recently formed Pop Scene Syndicate ("written by former teenagers"), advertises its features this way: "The younger generation has become a favorite subject of journalists . . . but with everything that is *about* them, *to* them, and *at* them, precious little has been written *for* them. Tuned in on what's really happening in the other half of the world, the Pop Scene group realizes what a difficult audience they're writing for. An audience that often criticizes the very devil out of something just to flex its intellectual muscles. . . . We produce *now* features that appeal to the restless imagination of the young generation by picking up the currents and undercurrents in the youth Meccas. At the same time we try to cop out our own big hang up—good journalism."

This may prove to be a stimulating suggestion for a local paper's column, if you're not a square. In dealing with this subject, you need to be hip and prove that you're tuned in.

Syndicates, like eggs, may all look alike to the novice, but they are not. Some specialize in feature material; others take only practical and helpful columns; a few are highly specialized and show an interest in only a few subjects. Very, very few are interested in buying fiction, or even reprint rights to it. To avoid a prompt rejection, observe what syndicated material is printed in your newspaper. Study the summaries in market books and consult such sources as *Editor & Publisher Syndicate Directory* and *N. W. Ayer & Son's Directory of Newspapers and Periodicals.*

Most editors prefer to see a minimum of two weeks' samples of a column; a few want enough for a month's supply—or more. Don't ask for a rejection, regardless of the value of your material, by sending in poorly prepared manuscripts or by failing to send a stamped, self-addressed envelope. Material may be typed like any other manuscript or mimeographed. If you have tear sheets covering published issues of your column, these are particularly desirable.

Perhaps after considering the slim chance one has of getting an acceptance from a syndicate, you will say,

"I'll syndicate my own column." This has been tried many times with but little success. A few writers have started on their own with two or three journals and then have been able to command the attention of a large syndicate. There are few success stories of this nature.

Your best chance of getting started on your own lies in personal interviews. Call on editors and convince them that your column will inform and entertain their readers. You may make your solicitations by mail, mimeographing copies of various issues, but busy editors are unlikely to pay much attention to or to be persuaded by this method, especially since the large syndicates send salesmen to call on editors. A smiling face and seductive voice can sell far more effectively than can even a well-worded letter.

In response to the survey of syndicates made by The National Writers Club, two syndicates reported that they had recently bought feature columns from free-lance writers, and another has some under serious consideration. The door may not be wide open, but it isn't shut and bolted. What are a few rejection slips on the way to final acceptance!

14

The Song Lyric Market

In one year, recently, the Post Office Department made 737 investigations of fraud by song sharks.

The temptation is great to become a victim of alluring advertisements and promises. Everyone knows that a fortune can be made by writing a song hit, and judging from those that are hits, it isn't really very difficult to write one. Who cannot rhyme *June* with *moon?* You don't write the melody, because that requires special knowledge and training, so you let someone else do that —for pay. All you do is write the "flimsy little whimsies," as successful song writer Lou Herscher calls them.

Writing for the song market can be heart-breaking, for it seems so easy. However, the fact is that this is one of the most difficult markets for the free-lance writer. Many of the large song publishers will return unopened anything that looks like a song manuscript. They have learned from bitter experience that the very simplicity of rhyming causes innumerable coincidences. These plague song publishers, who are often accused of stealing an amateur's song or a part of it. Lawsuits, no matter how ridiculously based, are expensive. Song publishers simply want to reduce the chances of becoming involved; hence the "returned unopened" policy.

The market is not entirely closed; there are loopholes. R. Gamba, manager of Pleasant Music Publication Corporation, tells you that "lyrics should be original. Don't write songs that have been written many times before and better."

You have to know what songs have been written and what now is on the market. Only in this way are you likely to avoid the trite and the obvious. By comparing what you have written, you may have a basis for judging your ability as a song writer.

A harsh but realistic command is voiced by Robert C. Haring, editor-in-chief of Painted Desert Music Co., who asks you to "write if real talent is present— otherwise, forget it."

Equally succinct and pertinent is the comment of Howard Zettervall, executive editor of Lorenz Publishing Company: "Learn English. Have something to say. Don't let the rhyming dictionary show."

According to *Writer's Digest,* there are 3,000 song publishers in the United States. (Some are occupied with selling only one song, written by the publisher!) There are 14,000 accredited song writers. Every week 200 songs are released under various labels. Out of these the number of hits is negligible.

Verily, as Tom Spinosa, partner of Dexter Music Company, suggests, "Treat song writing strictly as a hobby. If you have any talent, they'll find you."

Occasionally, the sun shines through the gloomy

clouds. A few song publishers, mostly those that specialize in rock-and-roll, ballads, country, western, and sacred songs, will at least consider unsolicited freelance submissions. This despite the fact that of all the publishers queried, only two think that the quality of unsolicited songs is good. All the others are of the opinion that, in general, they are unpromising or downright hopeless.

How does an aspiring song writer get a hearing? Naturally, the first requirement is a good song, both melody and lyrics. A query letter, preferred by about half of the companies surveyed, may bring a request to see the song, and this expression of interest is like having a friend in court. However, this open door is not enough, as Dirk Schory, president of Creative Music, so clearly states: "It is most difficult for a new writer to get his material established with a publisher with just a lead sheet. A demo record would help a great deal. Most of the songs we receive are very much outdated and not worth the time to consider them. A writer should study the market of recordings and published material carefully before submitting any new material to a publisher."

Archie Levington, general manager of Jobete Music Company, returns unopened manuscripts sent unsolicited, for, he says, "We do not evaluate unsolicited material submitted to us by mail for a number of reasons. Appointments for auditions are made by phone; however, we would not suggest making a special trip to Detroit for that purpose."

Other than the large publishers in New York and California, the song companies do not encourage sending query letters. A good demonstration record serves the purpose of an introduction and provides a presentation of the song.

The situation facing the would-be song writer is ably summed up by Syde Berman, editor of *Songwriter's Review*, who writes as follows:

"No list ever has been or could be compiled of publishers who do or do not accept material by mail. It is a hit or miss proposition. Many (especially the big publishers) do refuse regularly to consider unsolicited songs; others do and don't; you never know until the material reaches them. We have had a number of cases where publishers state they have an open door and want new material; yet, they refuse it.

"There is absolutely no standard. . . . The writer should contact the publisher first. If he has a sales talk —a song that is being broadcast locally, or that has been commercially recorded, he has a fine chance of being asked to submit his material. Many of the smaller companies, especially those in Nashville specializing in country and western songs, do accept material by mail.

"Keep in mind that publishers *do not* have a staff (such as do magazines) to review material by mail. They cannot afford such a staff, first; and second, they get a lot of material in person and through regular contacts. It is up to the songwriter to *sell* his song by letter. . . . *No publisher, to my knowledge, will buy lyrics alone.* Every publisher with which we have had contact buys complete songs only."

15

The Motion Picture Market

The brightest light on the literary horizon blazed gloriously for a historical moment and then dimmed to the point of obfuscation.

When the motion picture studios, well before the time of the talking movie, were considering original manuscripts from any source, would-be writers joined the "gold rush" to fame and fortune. There were bound to be similarities between scripts actually produced and ideas incorporated in free-lance submissions. Lawsuits, more nuisances than threats, followed. No longer would the film studios so much as open an envelope likely to contain a manuscript. The light dimmed, then went out. Only manuscripts that were sent by recognized agents would be considered.

Occasionally there seemed to be an exception, though all too often it was only a will-o'-the-wisp, not a rekindling of the light. A sensational tabloid carried what was purported to be an interview with the late Walt Disney in which he was quoted as saying he wanted writers to send in stories and story ideas. It was an "interview" wholly concocted out of thin air, reported the Disney Studio, desperately trying to stop the flow of unwanted manuscripts.

However, there appear now and then legitimate requests for original stories from free-lance writers without the intercession of the literary agent.

Sometimes they come from unexpected quarters. The famed director Walter F. Wanger says that he is willing to read unsolicited free-lance manuscripts and that he has bought plays from this source. In addition he wrote me as follows: "I was very much interested in your questionnaire for my own feelings have always been that there is an enormous future for writers in motion pictures. Our greatest cancer is the lack of writers.

"If a writer wants to write for the theater, he studies the theater and the proscenium for years and goes and watches plays and reads plays and, eventually, he is happy to get five hundred dollars, or a thousand dollars advance for a play that he has worked on for ages. Likewise, if he wants to be a novelist, he has read everything and he understands the technique.

"Regarding motion pictures, very few writers understand the medium, physically. The opportunities in cutting, lighting and effects are spectacular. Every writer, when he is a writer for motion pictures, should understand something about cutting. He should go into the cutting room and realize that the less dialogue used the better and the more action and more effects used will help to make the points. It is absolutely unbelievable to realize how little dialogue films have. Studying the finished film scripts would be of great value to people who want to write for films . . . in my opinion."

The kind of dedication Mr. Wanger recommends makes writing for the motion picture market one of the most difficult tasks an author can undertake. Few writers have the self-confidence and the pertinacity to maintain the regime required.

The failure of writers to understand what is actually required of a writer is a point made by William Grefe, producer-director of Zenith Pictures International. He advises the writer not to "be so talky. Most young writers make screenplays read like stage plays. Think up business that moves the story." This studio, also, will read unsolicited manuscripts if release forms are sent with them.

Jerry Denby, president of Vogue International Pictures, adds this comment: "Say it visually. Learn how to write good dialogue and use the dialogue sparingly. Don't get too involved in camera directions. Be original in concept and with characterizations. Don't copy what is currently being done. Think what would have appeal six to twelve months from now."

Most of the story editors suggest that you make sales in other media and then, with the help of a recognized agent, offer to sell the screenplay rights to the film companies. As Frank McKenna, assistant story editor of Metro-Goldwyn-Mayer, succinctly says, "Get an agent. Get published (you earn more money that way). Get to see as many pictures as possible. Get busy."

The easiest point of entry to the films is through sales of subsidiary rights to published short stories and novels. Not every novel need be a "best seller" to attract the attention of film moguls. Robert L. Flynn's first novel, *North to Yesterday*, was bought by Seven Arts almost simultaneously with publication of his book.

Another first novel, *The Dirty Dozen* by E. M. Nathanson, was bought by Metro, and became one of the season's most vaunted movies.

If you are a "big-name writer" like Elia Kazan, you can get an advance payment of $500,000 for the movie rights to your book, as he did for his novel (his first). In addition he shares in the profits of the film, which may net him another $500,000.

Even a nonfiction book may be salable to the studios. Some years ago Producer Pat Duggan told me he wanted to buy the film rights to Dale Carnegie's *How to Win Friends and Influence People*, but he learned that another company had already acquired these rights.

More recently, the nonfiction book *Is Paris Burning?*, coauthored by Larry Collins and Dominique Lapierre, was used as the basis for a picture of the same name by Transcontinental Films, Seven Arts, and Paramount.

Though the large film studios rarely will read manuscripts unless they are sent by recognized agents, some of the smaller companies will. A few story editors report they will consider unsolicited free-lance submissions. Among these are Vogue Pictures International, Zenith Pictures International, and Crown International Pictures. Interest in buying screenplays may be as temporary as a politician's preelection promises, so it is always well to check with the studio before submitting a manuscript.

The smaller studios are mainly interested in sensational, low-budget stories, preferably those that can be produced at a cost of not more than $200,000.

Anyone ambitious to write for motion pictures will not be intimidated by the obstacles to success but will watch for announcements of studios willing to read unsolicited free-lance manuscripts, or, if possible, will get a job, almost any job, with a film studio. With a foot in the door it is more likely that he can push all the way in.

The movies are here to stay. Though opportunities for writers may vary with each wind of change, the outlook is overwhelmingly difficult or bleak only for those who, possessing talent, give up too easily.

16

The Stage Play Market

What can be more satisfying and exciting than to see your story acted on a stage! How alluring to write for Broadway and earn all that money!

Many writers have tried to hitch their wagon to this star. Unfortunately, there is no more heart-breaking and elusive goal in the whole area of creative writing.

Convincing professional producers and little theater groups that your play should be staged is extremely difficult. Our survey of 35 producers of various kinds of plays reveals that of a total of 3,517 submissions of manuscripts in one year, only 23 were optioned or actually put on the boards. The percentage of acceptances was a mere .0065!

The producers themselves are pessimistic about the possibilities of an aspiring playwright getting his work accepted. More than 75 percent of them rated his chances from poor to doubtful. Nevertheless, only two producers thought that would-be playwrights should be discouraged.

The stage needs new blood, and there are those who

offer encouragement, like Spofford J. Beadle, vice-president of Producing Managers Company of New York City, who says, "We *need* you. But learn your craft and gain all the experience in and around the theater you possibly can. Keep working, reading, experiencing all the theater possible."

Talented playwrights should not be discouraged—even in the face of seemingly insurmountable obstacles. A realistic and sympathetic appraisal is voiced by Daniel Hollywood, president of Daniel Hollywood Associates of New York City, when he asks and answers the puzzling question, "What can you say to someone who feels the need of such expression? Thousands upon thousands of plays are written each year. Of these possibly 50 or 60 are optioned for Broadway, or for off-Broadway. Of the ones optioned, only a handful get on—for various reasons. Of these, you can count the hits on one hand (a hit, incidentally, is the play that repays its investors and makes some profit for the producer—nothing else is a hit).

"There is no frank advice you can give aspiring playwrights. If persons want to write, they all write and take their chances. I do, however, feel that a writer should be an *aware* person, tuned in to other people. Anticipate trends, analyze coming events before they are completely manifest. Most writers tell the same story over and over, though camouflaged. Writers are motivated by some deep probing of their subconscious. Their degree of expression is generally measured by their own understanding of it, and this varies in great degree. I feel that writers should read a great deal of poetry, study it carefully, learn the English language. Study the technique employed by successful playwrights and then adapt a style of their own—and having done this—find something to write about of interest to other people. Most writers feel that their own personal little Gethsemane is of vital interest to the whole world. Then their egos are wounded when it isn't so."

Another producer sums up the faults found in a great many free-lance manuscripts as "amateurish writing and plotting, cliché characterizations, and *polemicizing.*"

The majority of producers listed these frequent faults in the work of aspiring playwrights: weak motivations of characters, lack of entertainment values, unrealistic relationships among the characters, and the conflict not sharply delineated.

The consensus regarding the best way to learn how to avoid these and other faults is stated by Walter Fried, producer of *Death of a Salesman, The Man from La Mancha,* and other hits: "Get attached to a theater group! And remember if a scene or play doesn't work, it's not the audience's fault."

Brad Kearny, manager of the script division of Interval Artists Music Corporation, New York City, offers the same advice. "Work with a theater group—any theater group. First *read* a great diversity of plays. Study their structure and read dialogue aloud to 'get the feel of it.' And see as many plays (not films or television plays—unless that is the field in which you are exclusively interested)—and write!"

Just what you might do in connection with a theatrical group is explained by Tunc Yalman, artistic director of the Milwaukee Repertory Theater: "Work in the theater as actors, assistant stage managers, apprentices or what have you. Try to watch professional rehearsals to be sure that the material you have in mind is right for the stage."

A somewhat different recommendation is made by Philip Langner, president of the Theatre Guild of New York City: "Our advice to playwrights is to seek work in television or motion pictures. For every play that is produced, there are hundreds of television and motion picture scripts sold. A playwright can then learn the medium while working at his craft and getting paid for it. After he has mastered the aspects of character, motivation, plotting, etc., he can go into the far more difficult field of playwriting—more difficult to achieve artistically and more difficult to succeed in."

Allen Whitehead, president of Frank Productions, New York City, sums up as follows: "Learn your trade from as many points of view as possible."

What equipment do you need to be a successful playwright? The resounding answer is *talent.* Of course, this requirement is no less important in any other field of writing, but because of the expense involved in producing a play, talent is even more imperative in playwriting. Max Liebman of Max Liebman Productions, producer of stage and TV spectaculars, tells you to "ascertain from reliable objective sources whether you have any talent. If you receive professional encouragement, let nothing stop you." Or, as Shepard Traube, New York producer of musicals, dramas and comedies, admonishes, "Be born with talent! Is the writer really a writer? Does he have any gift for the theater? Can he write for the theater? And don't confuse the urge to write with talent!" Mr. Traube also gives advice on what to write. He says, "Write about something you know or have experienced. Write

about the world that exists. The number of acts in a
play script don't matter a damn; just is it a vital and
working manuscript. That's what counts."

Most producers, somewhat more than 50 percent of
those queried, will consider manuscripts only when
submitted by a recognized agent. Others have no objec-
tion to receiving play scripts unsolicited, directly from
writers. Nevertheless, it is advantageous to query a
producer before sending in your manuscript.

The hard facts of writing for the theater are clearly
outlined by William Hunt, New York producer and
director, who realistically says that "theater is now a
business. A producer must believe that a given play can
be a financial as well as a critical success. Reputable
producers will not produce a play they believe is not
good, even if the playwright should have all the financial backing for such a production. A producer's reaction to a play is purely personal. Every Broadway
producer turned down *Scuba Duba,* which is why an
off-Broadway producer got a chance to do it. He obviously believed the play could be a financial success,
and he was right. All the others were wrong. There is
nothing wrong with 'keeping the faith' on a play even
after it has been rejected by a great many people, but it
is best to write another play rather than to keep waiting
for the first one to get produced.

"Send plays to agents first. If an agent wants to handle
you, you have a much better chance to have your play
sold. Don't expect quick reactions or any reaction or to
have your script returned. Agents could go broke on
postage alone, were they to have to pay to return every
script they are sent.

"If your play has a great role for a particular star,

send the play directly to that star. If the star likes it, he or she can get a producer for it in all likelihood. If it is a movie star, he or she may decide to buy it for a film, although it may never get done on a stage.

"Chances are that if you show talent, though the particular play you send is not what the agent or producer wants, you will get a letter of encouragement and a request to see your future work. Follow through on these.

"Get any kind of production of your play that you can: amateur, semipro, college, high school. Audience reaction can tell you a lot about your script. Sometimes the reviews may even help. Never believe what your family, friends or associates say. They *cannot* be objective.

"Remember that you are competing with perhaps a hundred or so playwrights who have been produced, who are continuing to write and who have a limited market. . . . In order for a young playwright to sell he must have written not just an acceptable play, but a superior one."

When you have a play written, do all you can to get it produced—anywhere and under whatever conditions that may exist. "Try to have your play presented as a means of learning more about the theater and how the play must function in theatrical form," says Robert E. Dubberley, executive producer of the Charlottetown Festival of Canada.

Another angle to the value of production is stressed in an article by playwright Ken Parker in *Writer's Digest:* "A play that's been produced is more valuable to a publisher but many playwrights don't believe this. They think a publisher isn't going to be interested in a

script that's been done by an amateur group. . . .
David McKay Company says, 'We are always looking
for good quality three-act and one-act comedies and
dramas *which have been tried out first in local productions.*' "

Occasionally new opportunities for unknown playwrights arise, such as grants, contests, or special productions. Help may come from Eddie Dowling, the
dean of the American theater, who wrote me as follows:
"Play writing is in my opinion the most difficult of all
creative writing. If you are seriously interested, write
to the Eddie Dowling University Theatre Foundation,
in care of Richard Fallon, Florida State University,
Tallahassee, Florida, Department of Speech and
Drama. We are hoping to line up the 50 state universi-
ties in a great circuit of theaters to tell the American
story. . . . Ours is a story the youngsters should be
proud of."

The type of play favored by most of the producers is
comedy, with serious drama hard on its heels. Musicals
and farce rate strongly. Most producers like the conventional division of three acts, though two-act plays
please many. Little professional interest is expressed in
one-act plays.

One of the seemingly unnecessary frustrations to
playwriting is the time producers take to report on a
manuscript. Only three replied that they make a
prompt report. Whereas most require from four weeks
to three months or more, eleven producers were frank
enough to admit that an indefinite time elapses between a submission and a report.

Grandin K. Hammell, producer and director of Dia-
mond Bar Players, points out some stern realities about

writing for the stage: "It is a difficult road to success. Theatrical groups in general are rather disorganized. I have known production groups, both professional and amateur, to think nothing of taking six to eight months to respond to a submission. Any playwright must be most persevering, and almost as important as writing a play is the promotion of its merits and the developing of interest in it with potential producers."

Better luck may be had with little theaters, since one or more exists in virtually every state of the union. In all there are about 300 of them, so that personal contact is not only more feasible but also more likely to yield a reasonably prompt report.

Nancy Waddell, executive secretary of APA-Phoenix, New York, says, "Prospects are not good anywhere, but the *good* playwrights will be found eventually."

17

The Markets Await You

"There is no limit to the impulse to publish," according to the *Christian Science Monitor*, "and there is no end, apparently, of money to finance that impulse. The only thing there may be a shortage of is new manuscripts."

Most editors, I am sure, would amend the foregoing to read a shortage of *good* manuscripts. All editors, regardless of their medium, complain about the vast amount of dull, trivial, hopeless material that daily swamps the editorial desks.

To avoid having your manuscripts classified in this manner, you must learn to curb your impatience to sell. Learn to write well first. Merely plodding through a great number of words has little meaning. It has been said that after you have written your first million words, you are a writer. Attainment of this status is not so arbitrary. How well I remember the Kansas writer, author of seven unsold novels, a vast accumulation of approximately the desired million words, and now launched on his eighth. Alas, it too was unsalable, because he had undergone a process of adding words to words without attaining improvement.

How can you tell whether you really are equipped to be a writer? The understanding must come from you. Even your instructor in creative writing may not be counted on to tell you. Hatcher Hughes, the Pulitzer Prize-winning playwright and former instructor in playwriting at Columbia University, told me about a student he had in one of his classes. The man wrote several plays, all bad. He asked his instructor if his work showed promise. The dejected student was told he would do better to seek some other occupation; he simply was not a playwright. That student was Elmer Rice, who later became the author of several notable hits, including the Pulitzer Prize-winning play, *Street Scene*. Hughes swore that never again would he tell anyone that he could or could not succeed at playwriting.

You can get a key to your deep, abiding impulse to be a writer if you find that you can write despite rejection slips and if each such printed form is a command to reappraise your script and to rewrite it if necessary. A certain kind of courage and perspicacity are required to do what Richard Bradford, author of *Red Sky at Morning*, was prompted to do. After he had completely written his first novel, he put it away for a "cooling-off" period. On rereading it, he was convinced it was not a good story, so he burned the manuscript without ever sending it to a publisher! His next novel, constructed on the ashes of the first, was accepted by Lippincott the first time out. When you can see clearly the faults and virtues of your work—and do better the next time—you can feel reasonably sure that you possess at least some of the attributes of talent.

When you have talent, encouragement will come. The publisher Horace Liveright paid Sherwood Anderson $100 a week for five years and promised to take whatever he wrote. The firm of Farrar and Rinehart paid Hervey Allen $150 a month so that he could finish the novel on which he was working. He received a total of $4,350 in advance royalties for his unfinished book which turned out to be one of the all-time great "best sellers," *Anthony Adverse*.

All editors, as well as book publishers, are eager to encourage those writers who show aptitude for writing acceptable manuscripts. Whether or not you possess obvious talent, you can gain the respect of editors by sending them carefully thought out material. Prepare it in a professional way and direct it intelligently to a plausible market.

Editorial respect can lead to editorial assistance. And when you sell your first manuscripts, you may well be called to do special assignments.

Discouraging as rejection slips may be, they are facts of life. You are almost certain to get your quota of them, no matter how talented you may be. I know of only one writer who claims he sent out and sold scores of stories and articles without ever having to experience the gloom of receiving a rejection slip. I fear it would be difficult to vouch for his probity.

There is a vast and growing market for all kinds of manuscripts. At the same time there is an increasing editorial demand for competent if not outstanding work. The candidates for successful authorship are those who are conscientious and prideful of their workmanship. These are the ones against whom you must compete.

In all publishing and producing areas, from the modest to the most discriminating and demanding, editors eagerly look to the work of new writers. How else can they continue to function when established authors pass on? However, today there are no "easy" markets. Editors no longer will accept careless writing and warmed-over ideas.

It is important to every writer to have some idea of the market that is to be his goal. It is a personal decision that should not be influenced too much by the opinion of others. Now and then a university instructor in creative writing is disdainful of the smaller commercial markets. His gaze is on the distant azure hills of the quarterlies and the vast-circulation magazines. More realistic and constructive is the teacher who understands the aims of those of less ability. Some writers find satisfaction in entertaining and enlightening children or in getting into print in religious journals or even in one's local newspaper. Where there are pages to be filled with stories, articles, poems, and fillers, writers are needed to supply the material. It is not for anyone to denigrate the attainments of modest ability so long as they are achieved through the best efforts of which the writers are capable.

There is no royal road to success. Some seek the way by writing anything that may sell, patiently adding "credits" to impress an editor (and themselves). The intent is to make each sale a paving block that will build the road to success. Others may disdain this process and strike out directly for the desired goal, ignoring the satisfaction of traveling over the more secure detours.

Whichever method you choose, it is well to know that every goal can be attained, for no door is closed to the talented.

Work to improve your writing and you can be moderately relaxed about eventualities. When progress comes slowly or even painfully, regard what Jonathan Swift wrote:

> Blot out, correct, insert, refine,
> Enlarge, diminish, interline;
> Be mindful, when invention fails,
> To scratch your head and bite your nails.

Index to Subjects

Agents, 1-10, 18, 79, 98, 109, 111, 127, 128, 129, 136
Appearance of manuscript, 4
Article market, 26, 38, 41, 53, 66, 67, 74, 91, 97, 104, 107, 118, 143
  how-to, 45, 53
Assignments, 100, 107-8, 142

Books, 9, 38, 76-88

Children, writing for, 11-21
Columns, 118, 121
Comedy, 109, 138
Confession story magazine market, 1, 8, 60-66
Consumer magazine market, 8, 96-108
Controversial subjects, 18-19, 70
Coordinating Council of Literary Magazines, 38
Craftsmanship, 20-21, 54, 75, 84, 118, 143
Criticism, 41

Demonstration records, 125-26
Drama, 109, 138

Educational magazines, 8-9
Essays, 41, 97
Ethics, 49, 124

Farce, 138
Features, 53, 97, 117, 122
Fiction, 32, 41, 66, 67, 75, 79, 91, 97, 99, 104, 121
Fillers, 26, 67, 75, 91, 97, 143
Free-lance writers, 18, 32, 37, 39, 44, 52, 53, 69, 74, 90, 92, 94, 107, 114, 117, 122, 128

Greeting card market, 7, 55-59

Humor, 103

Illustrations, 74-75, 120

Juvenile magazines, 1, 6-7, 11-21

Lawsuits, 124, 127
Letters of rejection, 5-6, 39
Literary agents, see Agents
Literary magazine market, 7, 33-41
Little theaters, 132, 139

Markets,
  closed to direct submissions, 9-10
  knowledge of, 1-10, 19
  noncompetitive, 6-7
  strongly competitive, 7-9
Men's magazine market, 8, 67-75
Motion picture market, 9-10, 127-31
Musicals, 138

National Writers Club, 18, 56, 101, 107, 122
Newspaper syndicate market, 9, 116-22
Nonfiction, 79, 99

Outdoor magazines, 67, 70-74

Paperbacks, 76
Payment, 6-7, 33, 37-38, 41, 53, 74, 96, 97, 101, 107, 118, 130
Photographs, 70, 74, 93
Plagiarism, 114

Index to Publishers and Publications